REIKI AWAKENING

REIKI AWAKENING

A Spiritual Journey

ೞ೫

Dane Boggs

REIKI AWAKENING
A SPIRITUAL JOURNEY

iUniverse books may be ordered through booksellers or by contacting:

iUniverse
1663 Liberty Drive
Bloomington, IN 47403
www.iuniverse.com
1-800-Authors (1-800-288-4677)

ISBN: 978-1-4759-4773-1 (sc)
ISBN: 978-1-4759-4774-8 (hc)
ISBN: 978-1-4759-4772-4 (e)

Library of Congress Control Number: 2012916455

Print information available on the last page.

iUniverse rev. date: 06/09/2020

DISCLAIMERS

The information, ideas, and suggestions in this book are not intended as a substitute for professional advice. The author is not a health-care provider or doctor and is not qualified to dispense medical advice. Do not substitute anything in this book for treatment by a medical doctor or mental health professional. Reiki will support any form of therapy and is ideal for complementing medical and nonmedical practitioners. Neither the author nor the publisher shall be liable or responsible for any loss or damage allegedly arising as a consequence of your use or application of any information or suggestions in this book.

Rife machines are not medical devices and are not approved by the FDA. The use of Rife technology is experimental and at your own risk. If you decide to experiment with Rife machines, please consult with your trusted licensed physician, as well as a professional electrician or electrical engineer. The efficacy of Rife machines to treat Lyme disease and Huntington's disease is unproven. There are no published, peer-reviewed, controlled studies on the effectiveness of this technology in treating these diseases. Using any form of Rife therapy can cause a Jarisch-Herxheimer reaction, known as a healing reaction. These reactions can be serious and/or fatal. Any Rife machine user assumes the risk of a severe Jarisch-Herxheimer reaction. Neither the author nor the publisher accepts any responsibility for the reader's use of Rife technology and Rife machines.

To Lefty, our beloved yellow Labrador.
To my Channel and Ivo.

CONTENTS

FOREWORD

Every soul is uniquely significant. That is what Dane conveys so beautifully in the telling of his journey. With these words, he encourages each of us to listen to our hearts and follow our own truth.

Thank you for allowing us to be part of your process.

My Channel and Ivo.

PREFACE

My Reiki awakening occurred on September 3, 2007. On that day, I experienced a miracle. My life changed forever in those few minutes. This book chronicles my spiritual transformation in this life. Everything in this book is true, pure, and absolute.

My soul chose Lyme disease and Huntington's disease as a vehicle for spiritual growth. I achieved complete recovery from Lyme disease using alternative methods: Rife machines, Reiki, and spiritual guidance. This book focuses on the miracles I experienced and the lessons I learned. I want to share my story and provide you with an opportunity for greater peace, comfort, and bliss in your life. We do not need to suffer as we do. Become an enlightened soul. That's why you are here! You can take a train or a missile. The choice is yours!

www.reikimaster-daneboggs.com

ACKNOWLEDGMENTS

I want to thank the ticks that bit me. My path to the divine started with Lyme disease, so thank you, tick one and tick two. My first bite occurred in 1994 and the second in 2002. Lyme disease gave me an opportunity to find my path and awaken. I was diagnosed with the genetic mutation for Huntington's disease in 2003.

I also want to acknowledge the following people and spiritual beings for their assistance: to Dr. Kevin Holthaus who listened; to Dr. Bridget Freeman, for suggesting I might have Lyme disease; to my friends Lisa Barton and Mary Jaycox for helping me find a Lyme literate doctor; to my south Florida doctor who aggressively treated me for two years with antibiotics; to Didier and Ann Razon for showing me the world of energy through yoga; to Dr. Mark Mihaly, AP, who introduced me to Rife technology; to Amy Layh, my Reiki master, for guiding the light of my awakening; to Cherokee Tsolagui M. A. Ruizrazo for her reading; to Marilyn Edwards for her magical words; to artist Pablo Riviera for his owl; to Pat Wallace AP who introduced me to Ivo and muscle testing; to Constance Wulf AP who brought me a new sense of normalcy via the Rife; to Georgia Winegeart for her energy energy clearings; Bill Barton for my freedom and strategic planning; to my editors, Dana Carpenter and Anderson Burke; to my spiritual teacher, Ivo; and to my guides Egan, Saul, Sotu, Mary, Anahua, Strom, Germain, Sulvan, Tatum, Newman, Jeffrey, and Evangeline, Mortimer, Alan, Sabu, Watu, and Sherwin.

And saving the best for last, my loving wife Aimee.

INTRODUCTION

My Reiki awakening started with a disease, or should I say two diseases. In 2002 I started having health problems. The first symptom was fatigue and then joint pain, neurological issues, and finally intestinal pain. I saw many doctors over a couple of years. They all said I was in perfect health and not to worry.

Just before Christmas in 2003, I was diagnosed with Huntington's disease (HD), a rare neurological disease I inherited from my mother. I was told there was no cure. As bad as this news was, at least I finally knew the cause of my problems. It made sense. A diagnosis of HD explained why I was feeling so awful. As you can imagine, I became depressed. I started planning my bucket list.

Fortunately the universe (God) led me to an angel of a doctor. She told me my symptoms had nothing to do with my genetic disease but with Lyme. I said, "What's Lyme?" She said it was an infection transmitted by a tick bite. My blood test for Lyme disease came back positive. Lucky me—*I had Lyme disease*. I could fight Lyme disease. I could beat Lyme disease. Can you imagine being happy to have a diagnosis of Lyme disease? It was wonderful news for me. HD was something I could deal with down the road.

One disease at a time, please!

I started my journal in 2004 to keep track of my process against Lyme disease. It took me three years to get well. I started by taking oral antibiotic drugs for a year, and then my doctor put me on a year of IV antibiotics. Since I was still sick after two years of treatment, I stopped the IV treatment and tried a Rife machine, a device that uses frequency technology to kill the Lyme spirochetes. Within twelve months, I was well. All my symptoms disappeared. I was healthy. The Rife machine saved my life. I wanted to help others beat Lyme disease, so my path ahead was clear. I cofounded the nonprofit NEFLA (Northeast Florida Lyme Association) in 2009.

Reiki also played an integral part in my recovery from Lyme disease. My Reiki awakening allowed me to download divine light on a daily basis. What more could a sick person want? Is there anything better than divine light? It boosted my immune system and healed me on all levels: physical, mental, emotional, and spiritual. The combination of Rife technology and Reiki healed me. Years later I asked my spiritual teacher, Ivo, "Could Reiki have cured me by itself?" He said, *"Absolutely, but that was not your path."* I needed both Rife and Reiki to get well. Both Reiki and Rife technology are valuable tools for dealing with all diseases.

I am so lucky and blessed to have beaten Lyme disease in 2008 using specific electromagnetic frequencies. In 2016 I started used specific frequencies for fighting Huntington's disease with success. You may wish to experiment with Rife and Reiki to be your best self. Complete recovery in some is possible if appropriate for you and your path. These diseases have enabled me to grow and evolve. Here are a few things I learned:

- You are a divine, radiant being of light.
- You are an eternal spirit.
- Love is your essence.
- You are here to mature as a soul.
- You are here to become more enlightened.
- The endgame is a planet of enlightened souls.

This book chronicles my spiritual transformation. Read along, and see if it can help you find your truth. See if you can become more enlightened. Take one step at a time, and see where it leads. One door opens another. Find more peace, comfort, and bliss.

I hope my story and Ivo's words move you into the *light*.

Ivo

God is not a concept. God is within you.
All that is, is within you. It's all self-possessed.

With an open mind and a trusting heart, accept all
gracefully.

IVO

Ivo is a spiritual being. His first words to my channel were, *"I am God light."* I met Ivo through a channel on May 9, 2008. Ivo speaks to her from the other side, the nonphysical world. He is a teacher of *truth*. Ivo's words of understanding, wisdom, compassion, and love are contained herein. I am so blessed to have him as a loving, caring teacher.

My sessions with Ivo start with forty-five minutes of energy work. I lie on a massage table, and Ivo guides my channel during the energy treatment. Healing takes place on all levels: physical, mental, emotional, and spiritual. During this period, my mind, body, and spirit are brought back into balance. I normally drift off to a peaceful sleep.

Spiritual beings of all types show up during the energy sessions. These might be ancestors, deceased friends, or specialty guides. My guides have been Egan, Saul, Sotu, Mary, Anahua, Strom, Germain, Sulvan, Tatum, Newman, Jeffrey, Evangeline, Mortimer, Alan, Sabu, Watu, and Sherwin. They each have specific and individual roles in my energy sessions. My guides help me to evolve. I am so fortunate to have their assistance. As Ivo said, *"There is mutual benefit for all of you. Everyone gets the assistance he or she needs. It's a very complex and complicated existence. Everyone has his or her own source of support, assistance, guidance, and direction. All matches are made in heaven. Everyone is regarded and cared for by many."*

Healings and releases take place during these energy sessions. I often release pain and trauma from past and current lives during these sessions. Physical, mental, emotional, and spiritual healing can occur at this time. Ivo told me, *"You are in charge of the healings and releases; we are only here to assist you. You decide what you are ready for."* I have no conscious knowledge of these events.

After the energy work, my channel and I sit in comfortable chairs and talk. Her eyes are closed as she speaks in her natural voice. First she discusses my energy work. She talks about what was healed and what was released. She also talks about which spiritual beings came to visit and assist. Then Ivo speaks on subjects of his choice. Sometimes he gives me a heads-up on a future event or possible conflict. Often he gives me an update on where I am and where I am going. When he's finished, my channel says, "Do you have any questions for Ivo?" I look forward to this opportunity. My questions often explore my day-to-day activities. I might ask, "Why did such and such happen?" or "Please explain this or that." Ivo knows all and is *all*.

Ivo can see the future. He can see future possibilities. For example, he might tell me something as simple as a dog delivering a message to me or protective measures I need to take. Ivo's vision has reduced my fear of upcoming events and has protected me from bodily harm. Ivo said, *"You do get to exercise your free will. There are different futures available to you, but you are fairly easy to predict."*

Ivo can also see into the past. For example, in a past life I was the captain of a small wooden ship. The ship broke apart in a storm and everyone aboard perished. Ivo said, *"You still carry a sense of responsibility and sadness. It's still out there over the water. The grief, sadness, and tragedy buffer your sailor's passion. You are not ready to let it go. You still need to heal. Otherwise it sits in wait for another time to heal."*

With this background on Ivo and my channel we can move ahead. I am so blessed to have Ivo as my teacher. His insight into my current and past lives has been invaluable. There is so much help available. *"You can ask for anything, but you only get what you need. You are never given anything you cannot handle."* Let Ivo's words bring you greater peace and comfort. See the big picture. Live a more blissful life. Become more enlightened.

GOD IS REAL

The reality of God first entered my current life on June 21, 2005. That's when my beloved yellow Lab Lefty passed over to the other side. His departure opened my heart to the divine. I saw, felt, and heard the divine over the next five days. Miracles took place that eased the pain of his death. My Reiki awakening occurred twenty-seven months later and confirmed God's existence to me. I have included the following journal entries so you can see this transformation of consciousness.

SEEING AND FEELING THE DIVINE (FROM MY JOURNAL)

June 21, 2005

I put Lefty, our yellow Lab, to sleep today. He was nearly fourteen years old. I knew his death was coming, but I was not prepared. Last night, he couldn't walk any farther. Aimee and I carried him upstairs to our room and placed him by our bed. He seemed very sad. In the morning, there was no sound from him. He was in the same spot, but he wasn't moving his tail. He made no effort to get up. We grabbed a towel and placed it under his belly to get him outside. I guess that's when we started to panic. We called our vet, Herb, and he told us to bring Lefty down to the clinic. Two friends dropped by, and we all started crying as we loaded Lefty into the back of my Jeep.

On the way to the clinic, something told me to take Lefty to the beach. I found a spot on a small dune so he could see the water. We lifted him out of the Jeep and helped him stand up by himself. A shaft of light came down out of the early-morning sky and settled over the three of us. Lefty managed to walk to the bushes a few feet away and relieve himself. Aimee looked happy and optimistic.

I said, "This doesn't change anything. We can't go through this again. You know what we need to do."

Lefty circled the Jeep and stood facing the ocean. His ears lifted away from his face in the breeze. I could see him smelling the ocean. The years seemed to disappear. He was no longer an old dog but proud and majestic. He was in all his glory. The pain and angst in my heart seemed to melt. It was a magical moment for all of us, yet Lefty and I knew this was his last time at the beach. I looked up at the sky, and the light was gone. We placed Lefty back into the Jeep and drove to the clinic.

Herb examined Lefty and said, "We can try another drug. He might live another week or two, or maybe just a few days. When dogs stop eating, they want to go." I knew I had to put Lefty to sleep. It was the right thing to do. As Lefty lay in the Jeep, we shaved his front paw. He was nestled against the wheel well, and I pressed my face into his head. "I love you, Lefty, but it's time for you to go to sleep." There was no pain and no jerking as the needle went into his leg. He did not move, cry, or moan. He just went away. As I hugged him, I felt something pass through my body. It was a strange sensation. What did I just feel?

Herb and I slid the gurney under him. I said to Lefty, "Come on, just move a little to the left so I can get this under you." He was dead. He was gone, and I was asking him to move and help me. Herb and I carried him into the clinic.

I asked, "Is this it?"

Herb said, "Yes."

I turned and hugged Lefty along the full length of his body. "Good-bye, Lefty," I said, and then I walked away. I felt awful. What had I just done?

Reflections

I was in pain for several weeks after putting Lefty to sleep, but the pain was mitigated by wondrous exchanges with the divine. Lefty's passing opened my heart. It initiated tremendous growth within me on conscious and subconscious levels. Aimee and I both saw a shaft of light descend from the early-morning sky when we took Lefty to the beach for the last time. When the light shone down on us, Lefty was able to walk around the Jeep. Prior to that moment, he could not stand on his feet. This was God's blessing. It was a magical moment for all of us. We had just *seen the divine.*

As Ivo told me years later, *"It was important for each of you to say good-bye in that way. It was each of you allowing glory. Lefty appreciated his release. God's light supported the freedom of his departure and the healing of your hearts."* Later I learned that these go hand in hand. The more healing one's heart is capable of, the more freedom the departed one receives.

When Lefty died in my arms, I felt something move through my body. It was his soul moving upward and out. Lefty's transition to the nonphysical world provided me with an opportunity to *feel the divine.*

Ivo told me, *"You were finished with pretenses, with doing what you thought you ought or should do. You utilized Lefty's passing for transformation. Sometimes we use the circumstances, and sometimes we don't. It had everything to do with your position and availability. Everything you experienced was outside of pretenses. You began to identify with what was really real. The love and connection, the purity in that loss showed you what was real and what was imagined. Once you have glimpses like this, it makes a return to the past unsatisfactory. Nothing is any longer the same."*

HEARING THE DIVINE (FROM MY JOURNAL)

June 25, 2005

Aimee and I rode our bikes this morning. It was a beautiful day, and we decided to ride to Lefty's first home, where he spent his puppy years. Our return was something special. We stood in the driveway looking at the old house. Within a few minutes, a large owl flew by us and landed in a nearby tree. It sat on a branch staring at us. A few birds started nosediving at the owl, but it didn't seem to care. Several of the smaller birds were bombarding the back of its head. The owl continued to hold its ground.

Why was the owl there? Why did it stop on a branch where we could easily see it? Why did the owl stay in spite of the onslaught of those little birds? I said, "Maybe the owl is trying to tell us something." Aimee and I both heard and spoke the same words at the same time: *"Slow down and pay attention."* We were standing by our bikes, shocked and amazed. Then I heard and spoke the words, *"Everything's okay."* The owl then promptly flew away. So what happened? Am I going crazy, or did we both hear and receive a message? Did the message come from the owl, Lefty, or some higher power?

Reflections

This event was our third experience with the divine in four days. The message, *"Slow down and pay attention,"* came from the divine. We both heard and spoke the same words at the same time. The practice of *slowing down and paying attention* reduces stress and anxiety in one's life, allowing greater personal balance. Living your life from a place of balance puts you closer to the divine. Knowing and experiencing God is a wonderful feeling. Balance can get you closer. These are words we can all use.

"Everything's okay," brought me peace with Lefty's transition because I knew he was okay. I had made the right decision in putting him to sleep. Years later it took on a larger context. I would learn the world is perfect just the way it is. As Ivo said, *"How could it be otherwise if all is divine? All is God's creation."*

I received practical advice and peace on that day. The owl was delivering a message to me. There is a God. There is a higher loving power. You are not alone. *"Everything's okay."* We had *heard the divine.*

Years later Ivo said, *"The value came from your ability to listen. It was not that the words were so profound. It was your listening that was profound. It* *was the moment when things began to **clear for you**. After the fact, there was a lot of second-guessing. Aimee's participation and presence allowed you to be in it in a way that was climbable."*

MY BIG DAY—ATTUNEMENT ONE, REIKI AWAKENING (FROM MY JOURNAL)

September 3, 2007

My Reiki master, Amy Layh, said it would take about five minutes for my Reiki attunement. I thought to myself, *Well, it can't be much if it only takes five minutes.* She led me to the front part of her office. The room was thirty-five feet by fifteen feet, with hardwood floors and no furniture. It doubled as a yoga studio. She placed a small chair in the middle of the room and said there were four steps and I was ready for all four. I closed my eyes, and she gently touched my head and shoulders. For a moment, I felt like I might cry. Then she squeezed my hands, and I became electrified. My head and heart started to expand. The pressure was extreme. I felt like my heart was going to burst. The walls of the room seemed to bow outward. Then another surge of energy entered through the top of my head. It moved downward into my pelvic area. My entire body felt like it was going to explode. I thought, *There is no way I can physically survive this.* Then the physical discomfort ended. I was still breathing. Amy stepped away. She was smiling. She said my potential to help others was great.

Reflections

I had no idea that my first Reiki attunement would be so powerful. Everyone's attunement is different. Everyone's attunement is divine. It was the most important day of my life. My life changed in those few minutes. I knew something miraculous had happened. Thank you God, thank you, Amy, for opening my heart to the divine.

Ivo told me years later that my attunement might have been overlooked if it was mild. He said, *"You were preparing for surrender. Your processes contributed to your availability. Everything had to be just so for such a transformation. Sometimes they are not as complete and concise. Your willingness created an opportunity for transformation, and willingness is the same as surrendering. Most of your positioning was internal. Great magnificence can be offered, but you must be in position to experience it."*

Over the next few months, I witnessed Reiki miracle after miracle. My enthusiasm soared. I offered and shared it with everyone. I was very persuasive. I would say, "What is there to lose? I won't charge anything. I need to practice. Please tell me what you feel." I had my hand in the cookie jar. Couldn't people see this was the way? Reiki is the answer. Reiki is Nirvana.

How can I transfer healing power to the other side of the planet? How did I become a channel for God's light? Reiki is beyond reason, logic, and rational thought. It's beyond time and space. It has no limitations. I am so blessed to witness and participate in these healing sessions.

Every time I give someone Reiki, I know God is real. The divine uses me as a channel for God's healing light. I am a conduit for God's love, compassion, understanding, and healing. The amount and type of healing that takes place is between God and the individual. Reiki is real. God is real.

MY JOURNAL

I started my journal on May 16, 2004, to keep track of my battle against Lyme disease. Little did I know it would become a record of my spiritual journey. See if it provides you with a different perspective on life.

With Ivo's assistance, let us look go back in time. His vision of these earlier events provided me with a new perspective. I no longer see my past as I once did. It is forever changed.

Divorce

When I was twelve, my brother came to me. He was crying. I knew something was wrong. Soon my brothers and I were sitting in the living room with our parents. They explained to us that they were divorcing. Keith and I were to move to New Jersey with my father. Richard and Eric were going with my mother to Washington, DC. Our parents said splitting us up in this way made the most sense for our family.

Reflections

My world flipped upside down. At age fourteen, I left Salt Lake City, Utah, and relocated to Highland Park, New Jersey. I traded the snowcapped mountains of the West for the smell of chemical plants. Moving to New Jersey was a shocking experience. How could the world be so polluted? Growing up in the West, I thought our country was one national park after another. Not true. As Ivo said, *"Everything provides an opportunity to grow and learn."*

A Bridge

My father dropped us off with our canoe along the edge of the Egg Harbor River. I didn't like the way the water looked. The river appeared to be everywhere. At fourteen, I was the oldest and sat in the back of the canoe to steer. Soon we were paddling through a forest of trees. I realized the river was in flood stage. I thought, *This is crazy. Where is the main channel?* As we rounded a bend, I saw our death, a concrete bridge across the water. There was nowhere to go. I knew we were going to die. "Everyone down!" I yelled, "Everyone down!" We pulled our paddles in and prepared to crash into the bridge, but there was no impact. Instead we slid into darkness—the cold underbelly of the bridge. Surely we were going to hit something. Surely we were going to tip over. But instead we popped out into sunshine. What had just happened? How could we still be alive?

Reflections

It wasn't our time to go. As Ivo said, *"Accommodations were made. There are no accidents. Departure is between one's soul and God. Everyone is on their way to departure. Some are near, and some are far. Each departure is fit for one's needs and goals."*

Toni

The car was filled with pain. We were driving to Toni's funeral. I was nineteen and a junior in college. My twelve-year-old stepsister had died a few days earlier. She was a passenger on a small plane that ran out of gas and crashed. During the drive, my father and stepmother said we were being punished. They said God was punishing us for doing bad things. The explanation made no sense to me. What kind of God would do such a thing? If I ever met this God, I was going to punch him in the face!

Reflections

Years later Ivo told me my parents were trying to explain the unexplainable. They were attempting to cope and exert some control. Ivo said, *"The term of Toni's life was absolutely appropriate for her. Everything that occurs is just. Accept it and find peace. A power was left in her absence. Her offering is to be cherished. Her departure allowed you and others to find a capacity for cherishing. When you can do it for another, you can do it for yourself. The concept of cherishing was engrained in all of you."*

My relationship with Toni has changed since her death. In the past, I only felt pain, but Ivo said, *"Identification with your sister is becoming more detailed, woven, and complex—multifaceted. An extraction of your pain as it related to her was handed to her and released. It had no effect on her because she's in spirit form. Pain is a human dynamic. She and you were very pleased with the release of your pain. Up to this time, you used the pain to feel your connection. Where you are now, you no longer need it. This is a triumph."*

Nervous Breakdown

It was a perfect fall day at the University of Utah, clear and cool. I stood on the marble steps outside the registrar's office. I had just dropped out of graduate school. What the hell was I going to do now? I started to cry. I was completely lost. How could I be so lost? Tears ran down my face. Then I started to laugh, laughing and crying at the same time. I thought, *This is crazy. I'm losing it!*

Reflections

Some people would say I had a nervous breakdown. Looking back, I can see it was not a breakdown but a breakthrough—a leap of faith. Within a few months, I found my path remodeling houses in Salt Lake City. I stayed on that path for the next thirty years. Ivo said, *"The moment itself was a clearing, as if you were wiping the slate clean. Everything that had been significant and important shifted. Your attachment to your history was reduced to create a transformation. It was a defining moment."*

A Second Bridge

There were three of us in the boat. My uncle and brother were in front. I was in the back, looking for drinks in the cooler. We were flying across the water. I saw a low concrete bridge ahead and knew I needed to keep low. I remember thinking, *I need to watch out for that!* But I forgot about the bridge and soon found myself lying on the bottom of the boat. *How did I get in this position?* I looked at my uncle and brother. They were talking to each other as if nothing had happened. Even though I was unhurt, my life flashed before my eyes. I visualized my head smashing into the concrete and saw my lifeless body falling off the stern. I was dead before I hit the water. Everyone ducked except me. Why was I still alive?

Reflections

Ivo told me years later, *"A big hand pushed you down."* I asked him if he meant God. He said, *"Yes. There are no accidental deaths. If it was your time, you would have died. It was not your time."*

Note

The journal entries below took place after our yellow Labrador, Lefty, departed on June 21, 2005. They are listed in chronological order as they occurred. Let us continue to utilize Ivo's assistance for greater insight.

Catch-22

I looked for a puppy in the paper a few days ago. There was only one advertisement for yellow Labs. A nice lady answered the phone and gave me directions to her home. Aimee and I drove over and looked at the puppies. A little yellow Lab puppy started biting my sandals. Two weeks later we took him home and called him Catch-22 in honor of our twenty-second anniversary. He's so cute.

Reflections

Later I found out that Catch was born on the same day Lefty died. Was it coincidence? How could the worst day of my life also be Catch's birthday? Catch has been a blessing and joy to me each and every day of my life. Ivo told me years later, *"Human perspectives can be limited."* I did not know Catch was being born as I put Lefty to sleep. Ivo told me, *"It was all arranged. You are surrounded by so much support. Understanding and clarity will come later."* Wow, this was huge for me!

Marilyn Sends Me Energy Long Distance

I had my first long-distance energy session today with Marilyn Edwards. She's a healer. She sent energy from Florida to Utah. She said, "The soul craves hopes and dreams. Try to experience yourself living in joy and gratitude. Put yourself in a place to experience this. Only very advanced souls don't need such a place."

Reflections

This was my first experience with long-distance energy work. It made me feel very relaxed and peaceful.

Divine Butterfly — Moab

Catch and I were hiking when I saw a large brown butterfly. I said to the butterfly, "Do you have anything to say to me?" It landed on a rock and said, "You need to help people." I said, "Well, flap your wings three times so I know I'm not imagining this conversation." The butterfly flapped his wings twice but was bombarded by a white moth and took flight. I said, "Wait, wait, don't go until you flap your wings three times." The butterfly did a U-turn and flew back to the same rock. "Now please flap three times before you leave so I know this is all true," I said. The butterfly flapped his large brown wings three times. I said, "Thank you," and it flew away.

Reflections

Communication with nature does happen. You have to be available. Remember, we are all one. We only think we are separate. Ivo later told me, *"This was a tangible experience of oneness."*

Diagnosing Lyme at the Gas Station

I saw Andrea at a gas station this afternoon. I noticed a rash on her face. I asked her, "How are you doing, Andrea?"

"Not that well," she said. "I'm on my way to North Carolina to see a holistic doctor. I haven't been feeling very well for the last couple of months. I've seen every doctor in town, but no one can figure it out."

I asked her to describe her symptoms. Before she listed the third item, I knew she had Lyme. I said, "Andrea, you have Lyme disease. That's what I had. You need to come to my house right now and get some information."

Reflections

Andrea tested positive for Lyme a few weeks later. Why was I able to diagnose her when the medical community failed? God put me in the right place at the right time. I cofounded NEFLA in 2009 with Andrea and Aimee Boggs.

The Northeast Florida Lyme Association is now called the Florida Lyme Disease Association and can be reached at www.flda.org.

Magical Words — Forgiveness

Marilyn suggested that I say the following to someone who had wronged me: "Please forgive me and all of my ancestors from the beginning of time for anything I may have done to contribute to our present situation. Please forgive me and accept my apology. I am so sorry." This seemed like a crazy thing to say. I asked Marilyn, "Shouldn't the person who wronged me say this to me?" She said, "No—just try it." I did, and I found these were magical words. Something changed within me, and my anger melted away. Thank you, Marilyn.

Reflections

True personal power becomes available to the soul when true forgiveness comes into play. Without forgiveness, there can be no ripening of the soul. Forgiveness is the passport to divine greatness and our spiritual evolution. When we refuse to forgive ourselves and others, we inadvertently deny ourselves access to the highest spheres of happiness. Forgiveness takes strength and courage, but the rewards are beyond imagining. Forgiveness is love in action. This is exactly what happened to me. These thoughts are from Dannion Brinkley and his book *Secrets of the Light*.[1]

First Reiki Treatment to a Person

I gave my first Reiki treatment to Aimee's sister. Her neck had been giving her problems. I stood behind her, with my hands on her head and neck. She pulled a lot of energy from me. I felt intense heat in my hands and a strange sensation in my heart. She said she felt much calmer, and her toe no longer hurt either. She said she had recently broken her toe. Reiki really works. I thought, *This is neat stuff.*

Reflections

Reiki does the healing. The amount of healing that occurs is determined by the receiver and the divine. The amount of healing has very little to do with me. Reiki has an intelligence of its own. It knows where to go and what to heal. For example, the Reiki went to her broken toe without my knowledge.

---

[1] Dannion and Kathryn Brinkley, *Secrets of the Light* (New York: HarperCollins Publishers, 2009), 46–47.

Crying Baby

A crying baby was sitting in front of me on the plane. As soon as I thought about Reiki, the baby stopped screaming. The baby pulled energy for about five minutes and did not make another peep.

Reflections

Reiki brings God's love and compassion to all living things. The baby felt this and found peace.

First Long-Distance Reiki Treatment

I just gave a Reiki treatment to Tamara in Denver. She was home, and she agreed to let me try a long-distance treatment. I knew it was working right away. I felt the pull in my hands. How is it possible that I can point my hands toward Denver and someone can feel it? It blows me away. There is no rational, logical reason why it works.

Reflections

It still amazes me that healing can occur instantaneously on the other side of the planet. There are no time constraints or distances too great for Reiki. God is everywhere, and so is Reiki.

Bubble of Light in Yoga Class

Everyone paired up in my yoga class, and Ashley picked me. We sat facing each other on our yoga mats. Our instructor asked us to connect energetically. I had already reached Ashley with my heart energy. I felt a strong pull, and within a few minutes I was surrounded by a bright light. My chest started expanding. Everything was warm and blissful. I repeated the mantra, "One, one, one," so we could become one. When we finished, she started laughing, and I couldn't help but join her. We tried to control ourselves, but it was too much to believe and behold. We had just touched each other's souls and spun around the sun.

Reflections

This was a magical moment for both of us.

Too Much Reiki Given

I gave a long-distance treatment tonight to Mary in Pittsburgh. That's why I have all this energy. When I give Reiki to others, I get energized for several hours.

The next day:

I am feeling a little under the weather today. I overdid it last night. The twenty-minute session was too long. I need to be more careful. I am hurting. Ten minutes is the max session I can deal with. I thought I could handle it. I was wrong.

Reflections

It took me a long time to understand my limits. I still make mistakes. Self-awareness is the first step. I have to stay balanced to be of service.

Johnny Lever

Ivo gave me a heads-up. He said, *"Watch out for the Johnny Lever. Be careful and cautious when you are using it in the next months. Sometimes things are unnecessary. Be present, and don't let your mind wander."* When I got home, I tried to find it in the dictionary. There is no such word.

Fast Forward:

I worked on my van today with Robert. The rear brakes were stuck, so we had to jack up the vehicle. I knew this was my Johnny Lever day. I knew I had to be extremely careful. The Johnny Lever was the car jack. After completing the work safely, I felt a sigh of relief. I had avoided an accident—or so I thought. When I started to move the van outside the garage, it lurched. I immediately yanked on the emergency brake. What was that? We had forgotten to remove the Johnny lever. We were still up in the air!

Reflections

Ivo can see the future and past. What a blessing it is for me. I was lucky to have his warning. Fortunately, there were no injuries.

Spiritual Guides Egan and Mary

Ivo said, *"Egan is a jewel that is precious and treasured. He supports you in the way you intended for yourself. He supports your manner of fruition. You share fellowship. He has been with you since your birth—from the moment your soul entered your body. Your soul entered your body eleven seconds after your birth. Everything he is, is what you need, and everything you are is what he needs. Otherwise your relationship would be very inefficient. The two of you always have something to share and to gain. You enjoy mutual and equal benefits. Egan is your helpmate. Egan is your balance. He possesses inherent qualities in your existence. He is your counterbalance. He's in you, not outside of you. His energy and his effect complements you. You are Egan's sole purpose. This position for him in this life is a different one; it is not common. Your interaction has been intermittent until this life. You have more to do."*

Ivo said, *"Mary is an angelic presence. She bares and shares her love with you. She has really supported you in bringing your feminine side into balance over the last six to ten years. Her light is very pure, strong, and maternal. Mary is not the biblical Mary. She is of that essence but is not that presence."*

Reflections

I am so blessed to have Egan and Mary as spiritual guides.

Dragonfly

Yesterday morning I went out to my Jeep and saw a beautiful dragonfly sitting on my steering wheel. Where did it come from on this cold January morning? Was it alive? I pointed one of my fingers and touched its body. The dragonfly did not move. Was it dead or frozen? I gave it some Reiki, and it started breathing. I slid a piece of paper under its body and placed the insect on top of some nearby bushes. When I came home, the dragonfly was gone. According to *Animal-Speak* by Ted Andrews, "If a Dragonfly shows up in your life you may need some fresh air. You may need to gain a new perspective. You may need a change. It may mean you are neglecting your emotions."[2] It went on to say, "The realm of the Dragonfly is Light. They remind us that we are Light."[3]

Reflections

How did the dragonfly end up in my vehicle on a cold January morning? It was not an accident. It was delivering a message: "Embrace change. You are light. We are all light." The quality of light one brings to the world depends on the one's purity and standing.

First Reiki Attunement

When my client arrived, I asked for assistance from the divine. I prepared myself and the room for her. It only took a few minutes to complete the attunement. Afterward she told me she felt warmth in her body, a rapid heartbeat, and a sensation in her lower spine. I tested her ability to give

---

[2] Ted Andrews, *Animal-Speak* (Woodbury, MN: Llewellyn Publications, 2002), 340–42.

[3] Ibid.

Reiki. Everything was flowing. Her hands were getting warm. What a miracle. How does this stuff work?

Reflections

I have given many attunements since this experience. They are all different. Everyone has a unique experience. People can practice Reiki once an attunement has been completed. The more people practice, the stronger the Reiki flow. As Ivo said, *"You want to establish a well-trodden path."*

Big Sleep

This morning I treated my client who has cancer. Within a few minutes, he started to fall asleep—a full, deep sleep. His body loves Reiki and needs it for so many different reasons. He's been coming to see me twice a week. He could use it every day. His body soaks it up like a sponge. Yesterday he told me he was stopping because his blood count had not improved.

Reflections

Some people do not recognize the value of Reiki. Sometimes the benefits of Reiki are not consciously known or felt. They may only occur on a subconscious level. I have learned to respect the decisions of others.

Energy Work

My Channel said, "Your left arm was broken when you fell off a horse in Scotland during a past life. The energy was splintered and disconnected. During our session, it was repaired and reconnected."

Reflections

So many things need to be healed and released. Energy work can heal without conscious awareness. We are so blessed to have this divine gift available.

Shark's Tooth

Catch and I went to the beach today. I asked myself, *When am I ever going to find a shark's tooth?* Aimee finds them all of the time. I have spent years and years looking, but I have never found a shark's tooth. I said, "I need to really start looking! Now's a good time to begin." As soon as I looked down, I saw one between my feet. My first shark's tooth! It was very large, with a perfect shape. It was sitting on top of the sand as if it had just landed from heaven. I sensed help from the other side as I picked it up.

Reflections

Ivo told me, *"You had assistance. Egan placed you in the proper place to find the shark's tooth."* Help is available all the time. It usually happens without our conscious knowledge. I was conscious of the help. The expression "helping hands" is true. Spiritual guides assist us in so many ways. This was a playful example.

Spiritual Guide Sotu

Ivo said, *"Sotu is a warrior chief. He has the power of a warrior and the wisdom of a chief. He is helping you to develop these attributes by resonation. Sotu's presence provides validation and support for you. He has such a sense of wisdom and true power. He has warrior energy and fierceness and is solid and secure. His position with you is divine, not aggressive or offensive. Visits happen all the time. It is all by way of your hand. You determine what you are ready and available for. You get what you need and what you are ready for. It keeps it true. It does not need to be on a conscious level. It does not need to pass through those particular filters. Do not limit yourself to the conscious mind. Put yourself in a ready position. The availability creates the access. You* and Sotu want to bring factions and tribes together. You want to create bridges between diversity." Sotu said, "I am with you, brother. We are the same. Our purpose and offering are the same."

Reflections

Sotu was a new spiritual guide for me. You also have guides. Ask for assistance. They are here to help you grow, learn, and evolve.

Energy Work

After our energy session Ivo said, *"The aloneness, weariness, and sorrow of Lyme was released from your body. The sorrow was deep-seated."*

Reflections

How fortunate I am!

Spiritual Guides Saul and Germain

Ivo said, *"Saul downloads and exchanges information. Saul is very scholarly, newly attested, and certified. Saul downloads directly into you. This does not go through my channel. The energy he is bestowing is precious and divine. He gives you what you need to feel secure. This has changed your interaction with yourself and the world. Upward mobility promotes a new standing—partially mine and partially Saul's. You both benefit. You are a good team, effective and mutually beneficial. You visit often. You are in nearly constant contact."*

Ivo said, *"Germain is a recent assignment to you. He will regulate your strides for proper timing. He will help you be where you need to be when you need to be there. He is steadfast."*

Reflections

Again there is more help for me. I am blessed.

Healing Heart

A client absorbed Reiki into her heart. After about ten minutes, I decided to quit and let her rest on the table. My intuition told me to leave her alone. When I went back and checked, I could see tears in her eyes. I held her hand and asked, "Are you feeling sad?" She turned her head to the side and started crying. At that moment, I remembered what Michael and Laurelle had told me: "Let it go." I said, "Let it go; don't hold anything." It was a release. Afterward she said she felt much lighter.

She had an emotional release. The healing took place with divine assistance.

Elbow Implants

Today I adopted a tried-and-true device. I now have *elbow implants*. These energetic safety devices prevent clients' releases and resistance from bothering me during Reiki sessions. They were installed today with the assistance of Ivo and my channel. I had no conscious awareness of this activity. Ivo said, *"They prevent the backflow of energy into your body when you treat others."*

Reflections

I never have to worry about taking on someone else's energy or release during a Reiki session.

You Are Always Safe

I was feeling lousy on the flight from Orlando to Salt Lake City. I was anxious, tired, and concerned about my ability to handle the flight. I opened up my crown chakra to fill myself with light. Then I heard the words, *"You are always safe."* I felt connected with everyone on the plane. What a wonderful thing to hear and know. We are *all one* and *all safe* for eternity.

Reflections

Ivo said, *"This was a **come-to-Jesus moment** for you."* He also said, *"When you die, you know you are safe."*

Timmy

Lloyd and I met at Alta this morning after Timmy's service. Our buddy had recently died of cancer, and we wanted to honor him and his love of skiing. It was a magical bluebird day, with fifteen inches of new snow. I kept saying, "Timmy would have loved this." Then I corrected myself and said, "No, I think he enjoyed it." We both felt his presence. He seemed to be guiding us to the best spots on the mountain. It was a special day for all of us. There was no sadness. We celebrated Timmy's glorious life.

Reflections

Ivo said, *"The connection between each of you was very evident. It was your own private ceremony. It was mutually beneficial and needed."* Relationships continue in spite of death. The soul is eternal. Relationships are not severed when the body dies. Yet, as Ivo said, *"When people die, they do not stay that age or in that place. Don't hold on to the relationship that existed at death. That was one moment in time. Don't get stuck to something that no longer exists. Detach, and let your loved ones' heavenly presence be more profoundly and beautifully experienced."*

Race Day

I gave Angie some Reiki on her knee this evening. When I placed my hands on her knee, they became very warm. She pulled a lot of energy through me. She said she didn't know if she could ride tomorrow. Her knee had been very painful recently. Tomorrow's fifty-mile bike ride is called Blood, Sweat and Gears. I plan on riding, but she said she would make a decision in the morning.

Reflections

Angie rode without pain the next morning. I rode with her, and she continued to thank me during the entire ride. She was amazed. I wasn't.

Bear

Catch and I took a hike from the campground this afternoon. It was a beautiful day in Brevard. I was compelled to take a left-hand fork in the trail. It led us to a small cemetery, with six graves and three headstones. It was a small clearing surrounded by magnificent trees. Maybe my body was buried here in a previous life?

Ivo told me I was led there by a man named Bear—a big, burly mountain man. He was buried at the site. Ivo said, *"It was his heaven on earth. He enjoyed your company and is king of the mountain. He knows of **all** else but feels he belongs there."* I was not consciously aware of anyone at the site. This all occurred on a subconscious level. How often do exchanges like this happen?

The Eagle

I saw a beautiful eagle while hiking near Lake George. The eagle crossed the valley in just a few seconds and then soared higher and higher, without ever flapping its wings. No effort was used. At one point I felt like the eagle and I were one. I was soaring freely and effortlessly.

Reflections

Later Ivo said, *"This was quite a treat. The eagle was working with **all that is** rather than separately from it. It's a great metaphor for living. Utilize your experience and surroundings in a manner that supports you. The eagle allowed you to sense your own possibilities."*

Little Frogs and the Moth

I came across hundreds of tiny brown frogs on my hike. I was careful not to step on any of them. Then I spotted a miniature moth resting on a twig. I reached down and rubbed its back. The moth flew a few inches to a nearby pebble. How did I see something so small? How did I avoid stepping on all these little creatures?

Reflections

Ivo said, *"This was because of your recognition of magnificence. You had the opportunity to recognize the significance of magnificence. It was a doorway to yourself and **all that is here**. Every little thing has its place. All is significant. You can't help but include yourself in it."*

Mary

My channel told me Mary came to visit during the energy session. My spiritual guide Mary was channeling a strong, loving energy to me from my mother, who is still alive. Is this a normal occurrence? Ivo said, *"Mary channeled your mother's love to you. You still need it. The lack is still there, and you still need the love. This will create a fullness in your regard."*

Reflections

My spiritual guide Mary channeled my mother's love to me. This was done soul to soul, without any conscious awareness on my part or my mother's.

Amelia Island

My Channel sees me camping. Ivo said, *"You are alone for a day or two. This is a vision quest where you are alone with nature. It is nothing elaborate. You are just being with yourself in an attentive way—very simple and bare bones. Do not use energy to create a plan and details."*

Reflections

I asked Ivo if anything happened on my camping trip to Amelia Island. He said, *"It marked a moment. It was similar to a ceremony. It created a circumstance of definition that was not created by trauma. It was a pause. You achieved what you wanted to achieve. The more willing we are, the less the tendency we have for harshness. You need not have conscious understanding around this. You had a willingness to respect that time and moment. It is an indication of the ease you are creating with your soul. The human response is often to **prove it**. You do not need comprehension. Ease with your soul allows you to experience more with less trauma. Acceptance, grace, and peace are better. It doesn't eliminate pain, but it does provide a broader perspective."*

Last Rites

Aimee told me her friend's mother had a miraculous recovery after receiving my long-distance Reiki treatment. Her priest had just given her last rites when I sent the Reiki. Shortly thereafter, she made a full recovery. I am so glad she is well again.

Reflections

Things like this happen. It has very little to do with me. It's between the receiver and the divine. They and God determine the amount of healing that is appropriate.

Three-Way to Portland

I just sent Reiki to three sisters in Vancouver, Washington. It felt completely normal to me. I couldn't tell any difference, so yes, it worked, and they all received what they needed.

Reflections

I love doing long-distance Reiki. It still amazes me that such a thing is possible. There is no limit on how many people can receive Reiki at the same time. There is no limit on how far it can travel. There is no place it cannot reach or penetrate. Divine light has no limitations.

Shoulder

Everything was fine until I caught my right ski tip. I saw stars as I landed on my bad left shoulder. It was a direct hit on the weakest part of my body. What kind of luck is that? I dusted myself off and made my way down to the lodge. How will my shoulder feel tomorrow?

Reflections

My shoulder healed completely over the next few months. Falling on my bad shoulder turned out to be the best thing. It's perfect now. When the accident occurred, Ivo told me, *"Your injured shoulder need not be seen as a tragedy. This can be a great life lesson. Human perspectives can be limited. Good and bad are human assessments in accordance with pleasure and pain. Everything in life that occurs brings about benefits. This will reduce your tendency to be attached. Attachment inhibits fluidity and movement. Detachment supports fluidity and movement. The lesson is to maintain fluidity and detachment so one does not limit the potential of one's experiences. Whatever one experiences at any given time is of the highest good. Where you choose to be with that is unique to your current position and circumstance. Recognize all things and circumstances as opportunities. They support the breadth and depth of experiences. It's easy to see when it is comfortable."*

Homework One

Ivo said, *"Write twenty things that you love to do that bring you contentment. They can be small or extraordinary. Then look over the list, and put a line through those you already have enough of. At least once a week, pick something, and do it for yourself. Give yourself the time and opportunity to do things that bring joy and satisfaction, even if they seem trivial or insignificant. This promotes extension and expansion in a broader realm."*

Reflections

What does your list look like? You are worthy of greater joy, satisfaction, extension and expansion. Give yourself the time and opportunity to do things that bring joy and satisfaction, even if they seem trivial or insignificant. See what happens.

Homework Two

Ivo said, *"List everything you wanted or needed from another person but did not get as a child. List things, words, gestures—anything that is and was lacking. There is no judging here. Compile and keep this list going. Then choose one thing off the list, and give it to yourself. It doesn't need to make sense or seem significant. There was a need that was unfilled. There is still a hole. Often we as human beings live out our entire lives with these vacancies. This is not necessary. One word or gesture can fill those vacancies. Everything you change in the past has a ripple effect into the future. Do these in your own way and in your own time. You are ready for this childhood work. You need to repair and restructure your childhood self."*

What does your vacancy list look like? Give yourself what you missed out on as a child. This will create a positive impact on the rest of your life. Fill the vacancies. It heals the past and makes you more whole. You are worthy of God's love.

Nationals

I gave one of my clients a Reiki treatment last night before nationals. She called me from her parents' hotel room. She was having a bad night. I sent her Reiki as she lay on the floor. The next morning she competed and became an All-American.

Reflections

Reiki gave her the balance she needed to perform at her highest level.

Bobcat

I saw a bobcat in my backyard this morning. What a beautiful creature. It stopped under a big sago palm. We looked into each other's eyes. I felt a sense of oneness. Then it turned and slowly walked off into the marsh. I had never seen a bobcat in the wild, let alone in my backyard.

Reflections

Ivo said, *"The eyes are windows to the soul. It was a peaceful encounter because of peaceful positioning. No one felt threatened. It was a pure experience with a true sense of coexistence."*

Colorado Squirrel

This morning I encountered a Colorado squirrel. We met on the trail. The squirrel was extremely vocal. We were about eight feet away, eye to eye. I admired him as he jumped from branch to branch. Finally I asked the squirrel to come down and sit on a nearby log. I wanted to know if we were communicating. He dropped out of the tree and scurried toward the log, placing his front feet on it in a cartoonish fashion. I said, "Thank you for being so entertaining." The squirrel took off in a flash.

Reflections

Ivo said, *"Isn't life divine? One can acknowledge the divine in the simplest of forms and circumstances. This opens many doors and gives one the opportunity to experience more. All is divine. Be a witness. Acknowledge the miracles. Be willing to accept the offerings. There are opportunities that surround us constantly."*

Docking

Ivo said, *"Your docking is nearly complete. Docking gives you an opportunity to invite more of your soul on board. You are now existing within yourself at a fuller capacity. You will be able to tap into more of you. You will recognize this new ease. You will have a greater capacity to participate. Growth and expansion support more soul in the body.*

"Typically when one reenters life, one has a greater capacity for more soul than in the previous life. The downloading of the soul occurs with the new body and new life experiences. Most often the shift and broadening occur with the new body. This is not so common in the middle of a life. Typically what you have experienced in the life prior, as well as what you have learned in the current life and interim afterlife, determines your new capacity. When you die—when the physical body dies—all the things you learned in that life and afterlife promote an opportunity to hold a greater capacity in the next existence.

"What you did is a sign of the times. Docking is being created and encouraged on earth at this time. This represents an advancement of humankind and an opportunity for expansion in the universe. It's an earthly dynamic, but it supports something much greater. Docking is another way to create a profitable and effective standing in this world for all. It's an offering for all. Earth is unique. There are specifics here that are distinct to this place. Each dimension has its own purpose. You will feel more energetic in six to eight weeks. There is some lag time."

The docking took a couple of months. I felt tired as the process unfolded. Ivo said, *"Expansion is a necessary prerequisite for docking. Docking then leads to more expansion. Life is a powerful and complex existence. Capacity has nothing to do with the size and shape of the physical body. It is not uncommon for the capacity of the body to be less than the capacity of the soul. It is possible to bring more of the soul into the body. This can be a trying process. This dynamic is out of the ordinary. It is less common. It supports the purity of one's standing. We are talking about the amount of soul the body functions with. One's progression allows the body to hold more of one's soul. This is a reflection of humankind's progression."*

Babysitting

Baby Luke was crying in his crib tonight as I sat next to him. I decided to send him some Reiki. I could feel him pulling and absorbing the energy, but he still continued to cry. Something told me to pick him up. Soon I was rocking him back and forth in my arms. Within a few moments, he was asleep.

Reflections

So why didn't the Reiki work? What made me stand up and hold him in my arms? Ivo said, *"The two of you reached terms together. This was a soul-to-soul communication. He had a very strong need. He needed to be physically reassured of his security and safety. It was what he needed, and you acted appropriately. Souls are not held to a physical chronological standing."* Our souls were talking to each other! I got the message and acted accordingly.

Dragonfly and the Beautiful Lady

Today I saw a beautiful dragonfly and later spoke to a beautiful young lady. I asked Ivo, "Are they not exactly the same—beautiful?"

Reflections

He said, *"They are pieces of art. See the beauty and perfection of **all**. Step outside the human regard of perfection. Everything is perfect, even if it is uncomfortable and painful. Be willing to see it. Don't get caught up in your* *chosen perceptions. Be open to the perfection of **all**. See the perfection that is unique and distinct to each. We have the opportunity to choose our perception of perfection. Each has its own place. All is just. Step away from judgment."*

Angel

Aimee and I are in the picturesque town of Dahlonega, Georgia. We are here for a hundred-mile bike ride called Six Gap. We need to find a place in the shade to park our car so Catch can stay cool. There are no trees at the start of the ride. After discussing our dilemma, Aimee met a young lady who offered to babysit Catch. Lindsey had just finished college. I politely refused her generous offer. I didn't want to leave my dog with a stranger. An hour later, we found ourselves reviewing our options, and we decided to call Lindsey. Before we dialed her number, we saw her walking toward us. Yes, this was meant to be. Too many things were coming together. I knew I had to go with it. She watched Catch at her house and brought him to the finish line after the ride. It couldn't have been easier. She was an angel. She radiated everything good and loving in the universe. We were truly blessed by her presence and assistance.

Reflections

Ivo said, *"This was divine placement. A need was filled. It was mutual. It was powerful for her to be trusted in that way. She was able to feel her own trustworthiness. You were the one resisting the offer. It was enough volume and substance to override what you thought was common sense."* Ivo went on to say, *"It will be a carried remembrance for all of you. It's not the longevity of the relationship that creates value. The powerful presence of the circumstances gave each of you something to take away. There was significant divine placement that occurred, and it suited and profited each of you. It fitted and benefited all of you."* Things like this do and can happen all the time. Be open and available to all the possibilities the universe has to offer. Step into the flow, and take the ride.

Spiritual Guide Anahua

Egan introduced me to Anahua. Ivo said, *"He's here to support your throat chakra and voice and to support your attunement and expansion in this area. He is here to help you to convey a certain pitch and resonance with all. We are talking about vibrational energy, not tone. Sometimes a person is called what he does. Anahua means willingness to serve."*

Reflections

More divine help.

Three Ladies

On my way to the airport, I stopped at Lillie's Coffee Shop to post a Lyme flyer. I met a lady who had just spent three days at the Mayo Clinic with her daughter. Her daughter was diagnosed with fibromyalgia. I suggested she might have Lyme disease. The lady asked me to come see her daughter. Within a few minutes, I was at her home and met her daughter, Francis, and friend, Megan. Both complained of being sick most of the time. I asked them to consider Lyme as the culprit. I told them about my battle with Lyme disease and how I switched to Rife and Reiki to get well. When I mentioned Reiki, I felt Megan pulling energy from my left hand. Megan asked if I was sending her Reiki, and I said I could feel her pulling. When I raised my right hand to Francis, she did not accept. I felt rejection. Francis said she didn't believe in such stuff, but Megan continued to pull as we talked. I knew I was supposed to be there. I also knew these young ladies had Lyme. It was all arranged. I felt blessed to be of service.

Reflections

Later I sent them information about Lyme disease. They have not responded. My responsibility is to make the offering. That's why I am here. Ivo said, *"A seed was planted. Do not consider it unsuccessful."*

Shangri-la

It's the last day of our trip in southern Utah. I see a beautiful side canyon on my left and feel a strong pull toward it. "Let's go up there," I say to my brother and buddies. I get no positive responses. It's off the main channel, and they want to press forward. There is no time to lollygag. We are on a mission. Four of us are trying to reach the chute—a narrow opening to the sky—on the Muddy River. Two hours later we reach the chute, but the water is too cold and deep to press into the narrow canyon. We stop and eat lunch. It starts to rain and looks like it might snow.

On the way back, I insist that we poke our heads into the canyon for just a quick look. As we approach the canyon, the sun comes out. Walls of vertical sandstone rise to the heavens. A small trickle of clear water flows out of the canyon. This is nice. As we make the first turn, we see a waterfall dropping into a pool of clear, deep water. I shout, "Look at this guys—*Shangri-la!*" We are amazed. A rush of inspiration and enthusiasm comes over me. I'm no longer tired. There are cairns leading us to the top of the waterfall. John and I scurry up the walls. Within a few minutes, we are standing above the waterfall. What a magnificent place. I see my brother Keith swimming below in one of the pools. Jumping from this high place sure looks like fun, but it is a long way down. John and I hike back down the same way we came up. It's slow going, and at the bottom we high-five each other in celebration. I need to come here again and camp in Shangri-la.

Reflections

Ivo said, *"It was a feather in your cap, something you will all remember. It is important to acknowledge that your whims need no justification, whether your reward is apparent or unapparent. Whims and inclinations are opportunistic. They come to you for a reason. You need not know what the reason is. They are soul oriented. Finding the valley was a reward for following your instincts."*

Jorgan

As I was leaving John's house, I went over to say good-bye to his dog, Jorgan. He was curled up in his favorite chair. I reached out to pet him, and I could feel him pulling Reiki from my hand. Jorgan needs surgery on his liver. I stayed and placed both hands on his body. He pulled a lot of energy through me. He needed Reiki in a bad way. After ten minutes, I disconnected.

Reflections

I plan to send Reiki to Jorgan after his surgery. I know it will help his recovery. The healing is between God and Jorgan. God does the healing and regulates all departures. I do not know Jorgan's path.

My Father

Ivo brought me up-to-date on my father, who died in 1989. Ivo said, *"He's nine years old and lives in the Pacific Northwest. He is nine going on thirty. He is very wise for his years. He's making such progress at a young age. He can steer clear of taking on another's burden on himself. He has very clear boundaries. He realizes it's not about him; it's about them. He learned it the hard way last time. His thirties were very defining for the rest of his life. He was very angry about the divorce. It's to each of us to choose our form of definition. Circumstances of great opportunity are always defining, but how we choose to be defined by them is ours. You can live in tragedy, or you can live and grow to implement changes in the world. We each make our pathway. It's a matter of choice. He was eager to right himself."*

Reflections

It's nice to know my father is doing so well in his new life.

Not My Path

Huntington's disease is not my path. Ivo said, *"It is not a defined dynamic in your existence. It is not a dynamic that you need to complete in this lifetime. Your heading does not include it."*

Reflections

Maybe this dynamic was experienced in a previous life, or maybe it waits for a future one.

I could depart another way. Timing and method are in the hands of God. Departure provides an opportunity to be with God, to review one's life, and to come back with greater capacity to serve.

Distracted

I'm upset at myself for getting sick. I feel it's my responsibility to stay healthy. My in-laws were here over Christmas, and I failed to define my space. I neglected myself. I put my life on hold. I cut myself off from the source—from God—and suffered the consequences.

Reflections

Ivo said, *"You cannot disconnect from God because you are god."* He went on to say, *"You were distracted. Their intentions, their situations, and their processes were a distracting energetic dynamic. Overextension and overexertion were experienced on your part. You let go of your covenant relationship with self. You were involved outwardly in an* unbalanced *way. It's all about gathering an ability to temper and balance."* In terms of the anger I felt toward myself, he said, *"It's so important to remain positive, supportive, and encouraging. Do not fall into a state of judgment. Do not berate or judge your previous choices. Simply learn from them. How might you choose to do it differently next time? It does not behoove you to turn on yourself in any way, shape, or form. To regret, to judge, or to ridicule a past position only creates distrust within yourself. Remain supportive, encouraging, and comforting all the days of your life. Acknowledge the progress you are making. All steps are important."*

I learned a valuable lesson from getting sick. Do not get distracted by the processes, situations, and intentions of others. Maintain balance and the covenant relationship with self at all times.

Prostate

I went to my doctor today and received disappointing news. My PSA levels have increased. The doctor wants to do a bioscopy for cancer. I told the doctor, "I'm okay. I'm going to have a gradual return to normal." I wasn't worried, but I could see he was. I told him I would do a bioscopy if the numbers didn't come down over the next couple of months. He agreed to wait.

Reflections

Ivo said, *"There is a lack of fluidity. The energy is stuck in one region on the south end. It is still true that you will have a gradual return to normal. You are not normal yet. Use acupuncture, etc., to move the energy and Reiki. There is no symmetry now. It needs to be a complete and vital organ."* When I asked Ivo about my new bicycle seat, he said, *"It is better. There is a challenge in the change. If you had gone from your old seat to the current one, you might not have noticed the change. But you went from your old seat to a different seat to your current seat. The transition would have been swifter without the different seat. Final change and adjustment are coming. It is not necessary to return your current seat and start over."*

I knew my new bicycle seat was increasing my PSA numbers. My PSA numbers dropped back down, and the doctor canceled my bioscopy. Nice to have Ivo in my corner!

Crown Chakra

I can open my crown chakra at any time by simply saying, "Open, open, open." It feels as if someone is pushing down on my head with his or her hand. There is a lot of pressure in and on the top of my head. It is not unpleasant but is noticeable. The top of my head feels open to the universe. It happens all the time, with or without conscious intent.

Reflections

Ivo said, *"It's always an indication of your preparedness. You have to be ready, prepared, and available for that to occur. It will not happen unless you are prepared. A variety of circumstances and opportunities are available, conveying information and energy; creating access and interacting with more; and engaging with other spiritual and human beings. Others cannot find you or find access within you. The door does not swing both ways—only one way. It allows you to be available for a variety of offerings. Your crown opening is distinct and specific to each moment and depends on your preparedness. It is valuable to accept this experience without control. It does not need to be by way of conscious consideration."*

My channel said, "When your crown opens, a bright pink light appears. Red represents the passion of the heart, and white represents the divine. Blend them and you get pink. It is evidence of passion with divine influence."

Big-Time Fun

Bea came to me for a Reiki treatment. She is a massage therapist and seemed way out of balance. She had been giving Reiki to her clients unknowingly. It was making her sick. I gave her some rituals to adopt for staying balanced and centered. I told her, "No more Reiki for your massage clients—only physical massages. Only give Reiki to yourself until you refill your personal reservoirs." I also told her, "You were born wide open. You were born a Reiki master, but you need coaching to stay healthy and effective."

Reflections

This is what I was meant to do. I love teaching. This session brought me so much pleasure. To stumble upon a Reiki master in the raw—wow! Finding someone who doesn't need attunements is big-time fun for me!

Dane Boggs

The Horse Whisperer

Here's an e-mail I received today from one of my students:

Dane,

I wanted to tell you about the horse that passed away. I was called last Thursday to come and see if I could help Selina (the horse). I went right away as I knew she was in awful pain from laminitis. (This is a disease that virtually tears the bone away from the inside of the hoof. If left untreated, the hoof will detach from the leg, and it was.) I did Reiki (even though I thought I had nothing), and the horse really responded. She stood up after lying down for two months. She stopped her pain responses, like licking the air and chewing her leg.

To the untrained eye, you would have thought there was hope. Actually, the Reiki was helping her transition to what needed to happen—her euthanasia. The Reiki made her more comfortable to get to the decision her owners needed to make.

She had languished too long in this pain. I don't blame the owners; they were relying on the vets, who were no help in making a final decision. I went every day, twice a day, to touch her. She touched me. I felt her spirit, her bravery, and her loving soul, and I felt changed.

Blessedly, on Monday morning she was euthanized. I felt her spirit leave her body, but she has not left my mind. I continue to cry over a horse I knew for a brief moment in time. I am sad for the horses (and other animals, of course) who do not have an advocate to help them pass and be free of pain.

I am fine … more than fine, I guess. I think I know what I am to do now.

Missy

Reflections

All life forms benefit from Reiki. Missy has a special gift. She eased Selina's pain and helped her make the transition to the other side.

The Walk

I spoke with Ivo about my walk in 2005. I couldn't sleep that night. My pain was so great after putting our dog, Lefty, down, so I went outside. By the time I got back to the house, all my pain was gone. I was in a state of complete peace. How did that happen?

Reflections

Ivo said, *"**You were bathed** by **all that is**. It lightened your load. You asked for help, and it was given. You were available and willing. You had been marinating in grief while in bed, holding on to the sadness. You were attached.*

*When you got up, you surrendered. You stopped trying to control and fix it. You let go of it, and it moved. Letting go allowed things to move and shift. It created movement for you. The air, the starlight, the energy, the moonlight, the purity, and the energy of nature—**you were bathed** by **all that is**."* Thank you, **all that is**.

Colorado Meditation

The key words for my Colorado meditation were open, input, restore, balance, grounded, and thank you. I also used the Reiki symbols. My Reiki meditation was much more powerful than at home in Florida. The elevation in Winter Park, Colorado, is around nine thousand feet.

Reflections

Why was this meditation so powerful? Ivo said, *"One's physical location has a great effect on what is available to experience. Every physical place has different energy. Everyplace has a vibration. The energy is lighter in Colorado. Your experience was broadened and enhanced. Eventually your experience out West would become less special and distinct."*

Titanic

I asked Ivo why the sinking of the *Titanic* pulled so much on my heart. Ivo said, *"You are profoundly empathetic. You lost those near and dear to you in similar fashion. A Norwegian vessel sank in your twenty-second life, carrying those you loved. Your empathetic quality wanted to know what it was like for them. You imagined them drowning. Your imaginings soon become memories. Once you imagine something, it is a reality and becomes a memory. Be conscious of your thought."*

Reflections

This was a biggie for me. Our thoughts, whether real or imagined, become our memories. These memories can be with us for a long time—many lives. Make sure they are positive in nature. As Ivo said, *"Be conscious of your thought."* Your thoughts become your reality, whether real or imagined.

Release

Ivo told me, *"You released entanglement during the energy work. Your right foot was caught in a copper coil."* I could not remember the event, but he said it occurred in a room with a plywood floor. Ivo said, *"The energy is now settled. The suddenness of the event created harshness. Emotional fragility and helplessness were released."*

Reflections

How much stuff do we need to release? Ivo said, *"Often releases occur by similar repeat performances. Those kinds of courses move through us in a nearly constant manner. We can empty our baskets as we move along. Life and living are all about taking what is available and utilizing it in a way that is divine for you and setting aside what is excess."*

Grafting

Mazie came to visit. She is on my mother's side—five generations back. Mazie said, "You are grafting the family tree." She wanted to express her gratitude. She said I am bringing something into the family tree that changes everything. Ivo said, *"This changes all those who came before, all those who are here with me, and all those who will follow—forevermore. All is not linear. It has to do with connections. There is always a connection."*

Reflections

I had no idea that grafting was possible. What we do in our current lives can have a tremendous impact on current, past, and future generations. Wow! The souls of my ancestors, past, current, and future, can be impacted by what I think and do *today*. Ivo said, *"The complexity is mindboggling—not comprehensible. It is not something the mind can grasp or position."*

Living

Ivo said, *"You have an interest in creating an awareness around the vast difference between living and survival. Survival is less vibrant. You want to help others experience the difference between living and survival. When one begins to realize the difference, survival is no longer acceptable. For many it is about realizing that it is available and they are deserving."*

Reflections

We are all deserving of this experience. Life can be vibrant, alive, and magical. Moving beyond survival is a wonderful thing. As Ivo said, *"Give yourself permission to experience living. This has nothing to do with what life looks like. We don't always sense our connection to the divine, but it's there."*

Limitations

I sent long-distance Reiki simultaneously to Rollie, Carol and Cile, all in different physical locations. It seemed to work just fine.

Reflections

Ivo said, *"Limitations are imagined. They do exist if they are imagined. That which is imagined can be experienced as absolutely real. You were exploring. You like the woods."* Anything is possible with Reiki. The only limitations are those we create with our small minds. God determines the amount of healing that is appropriate.

Ivo said, *"Your sense of discernment in relationship to opportunity and diversity is changing. You were more absolute, but you are now open to broader possibilities. Don't create a process or a system that is patterned or habitual that does not acknowledge the perfection of what is needed. Be in a way that allows you to negotiate. Nothing is going to override that which is divine."*

Passage

Ivo said, *"Sometimes passage is just passage. Different methods, illnesses, and accidents are at hand. The perception of a job well done can bring peace and satisfaction at passage. This is not always clearly identified until passage is complete. There is something very powerful about the human attachment to living. It is often needed to instill perseverance and determination because life can be hard. If humans didn't have this survival instinct, people would be leaving left and right. It's hard here. There is a human instinct that promotes perseverance and dedication when it is uncomfortable and challenging. There is a human attachment to living and survival that is a very integral part to sustaining the willingness to participate. Sometimes the instinct for survival overrides the soul's own awareness that passage is appropriate. You don't need to know you are ready to be ready."*

Reflections

Being human is no small task. Our survival instinct keeps us in the game of life. This provides us with more time to learn, grow, and evolve.

Spiritual Guides Sulvan and Tatum

Egan introduced me to guides Sulvan and Tatum. They wanted to thank me for helping others. Their presence was determined by an interest in conveying gratitude. They bathed me in gratitude, and I accepted reluctantly.

Reflections

Ivo said, *"Your ego had a difficult time with the offering of gratitude. Be in that gratitude. Saturate yourself with the offering. Embrace the offering. Practice. Receiving is a gift to the giver. Do another the honor by being in it well."*

Bird's Nest

I found a bird's nest in a flowerpot on the back porch. The baby birds had flown the coop. Ivo told me to expect such an experience during our last session.

Reflections

Ivo said, *"Their journey continues. One bird concluded life. Observe the process and cycle of life that is profound. There is beauty and perfection in every part. No one place or moment is better than another. Being in your twenties is not better than your nineties. Have reverence and respect for all."*

Hawk

I was mowing the yard when a hawk flew over my right shoulder. He landed on a branch in the backyard and stayed until I finished cutting the grass. Then he flew off.

Reflections

I thoroughly enjoyed the presence of the hawk. Ivo said, *"The hawk was drawn to the golden light of your energy. He was aware and curious. Your glow was more outstanding at that moment. The hawk saw it as a shining, golden reflection. Once he became familiar with it, he became comfortable, and this allowed him to remain. You coexisted on a primal level. Gifts were given in both directions. Something mutual was exchanged."*

Lower Back

This morning before I got out of bed, I gave myself a Reiki treatment. I normally do this for a few minutes each morning before I begin my day. I could feel the Reiki going to my spine. It was very powerful to the point of discomfort. I stayed with it for an hour because I obviously needed the therapy time. Now it is less painful.

Reflections

Ivo said, *"Your body was very receptive at that moment. It has more to do with your willingness. A surge of energy created active movement in your kundalini. You cannot override the divine. You cannot restrict it either. Be a part of **all that is** without separation. It's about allowing yourself to no longer feel separate. It's an opportunity to feel the fullness of self."*

Catch and the Little Boy

Everyone wants to pet our yellow Lab, Catch. Soon a three-year-little boy and Catch were engaged in a hugging contest. They seemed to be falling in love with each other. This went on for twenty minutes. They couldn't stop playing with each other.

Reflections

Ivo said, *"They were both enamored with each other's aura. Enthralled, mesmerized. Pure enjoyment of each other's purity."*

Cycling with Stephanie

I dropped off the back of the bike group and found myself riding with Stephanie. As we cycled together, we started to discuss our bad knees. She expressed her frustration with trying to get in shape. Her bad knee was holding her back. I said, "You need to be more patient! Why can't you give it time to heal?" There was a shocked expression on her face. Why did I say such a thing?

Reflections

Ivo said, *"It was passage of a message from Ione. There was very little thinking involved. No reason to question it."* Ione is a guide for Stephanie. It's what Stephanie needed to hear. The divine used me to deliver a message to Stephanie.

Rife Machine

I had some unusual sensations after using my Rife machine. Ivo said, *"There's no evidence of Lyme within your body, but there is cellular remembrance. From time to time it can resource that memory. Do not use the machine randomly. It is unnecessary to randomly engage yourself in the vibration. Be observant. It's an advantage for you to be aware. If you are not leaving the room, it's important to define your own clear space. It's all energy."*

Dane Boggs

Reflections

I use the Rife machine carefully and sit to the side when assisting others.

Evangeline

Evangeline participated in my energy session today. Ivo said, *"She is here to take your mother to the other side. Evangeline is honored by the role and your mother by her assistance. Know that your mother is in good care. This is not a specific role for Evangeline, but it is the connection she has with your mother."*

Reflections

It's reassuring that my mother's passage to the other side is in good hands. This provides me with a sense of comfort as she moves closer to departure.

The Complete Circle

Ivo put me on notice. *"You will be man of the hour. What you bring is received, and it is also important that what is brought to you is also received. Be accepting as well. Have a full experience. Shift gears and receive. Be there in a more balanced scenario. Be neutral and receive. Allow yourself to embrace that position. Comfort with self makes it easy for them. Be in it gracefully. All of the process is to be beautiful. Just receive."*

Reflections

A few days later I ran into Bea. She said, "You saved my life." This was the second time in the last few months someone had said those words to me. Ivo said this would happen. I hugged her when she said the words. I completed the circle by accepting her gratitude.

Awakenings

Ivo said, *"Typically in a life's existence there will be a moment of prominent return to awareness. The state of evolvement is dependent on one's processes. All factors are influential. Steps that we take are different and personal. The awakening is not a destination. It's not a shared moment or experience by all that exist. It's different, and it has to do with the momentum you bring to that place and the momentum that carries you further. Typically when one recognizes that moment in one's journey, it is a leap, a shining moment.*

No two are to be measured. The awakening has more to do with the step and range that is covered and one's ability to identify the existence of purity within that supports each in his or her own way in his or her own time. These are varying experiences. It's not so much about where one is but more about one's processes. It's the process, not the moment. It doesn't look one way. An awakening acts as a catalyst for all that follows. For you and most it is a new definition of real. It is distinct to the individual."

Reflections

Everyone has their path. Awakenings occur in all shapes and sizes. We are all here for the same reason—to grow, evolve, and become more enlightened.

Yoga Class

At the end of my yoga class, I offered Reiki to everyone. This was done on a subconscious level. I did not speak to anyone. Most people had their backs on the floor and feet up the wall. I stayed in the middle of the room and pointed my hands toward the ceiling for ten minutes. I could feel it flowing out my hands. Afterward my wife asked, "Were you sending?" I said, "Yes I was."

Reflections

Ivo said, *"There was a very open state of being in you and the room due to the yoga. You experienced yourself as a tool. Openness and fluidity allowed a very pure level of offering to occur. There was a level of trust that was invitational. The yoga class facilitated balance within you and helped you deliver a more pure and effective offering. Every Reiki offering is different. It need not be a formal presentation and execution. It was a value for you to be an observer. Much can be gathered from observation. Stand aside of assessment. It can be quite a roller coaster. Be part of the process. You were a facilitator."*

Night Sky

Ivo said, *"The night sky is magical, with no bounds! For you it's about the closest thing to heaven on earth. You sense, feel, and know your essence outside your physicality. Who you are. Your true essence. These experiences can be created in our minds. It requires a lot to exist in this world. A pure, unfiltered state of being is rejuvenating for you. Identification of your purity is comforting."*

Reflections

Soon I will be in the desert camping. I can see the clear night sky, and the stars are touchable. The thought of such beauty creates a sense of peace and oneness within me.

Wrong Turn?

I was driving, and Aimee was directing. We made a wrong turn. Ivo said, *"That jaunt was not a mistake, and you were not lost. The wrong turn was intentional and purposeful. It was about positioning you in a way that you are in the right place at the right time. You were running a little ahead of schedule. The jaunt allowed you to go back into your place in a more proper way. Often there are modes of involvement that support one's proper position where outside forces and influences involve in such a way to bring things back into proper timing accordingly. It put you back where the two of you needed to be to be in your most appropriate and effective standing."* My channel said, "It can be mind boggling if you think about it."

Reflections

The next time you make a wrong turn, it may be just what you needed to maintain proper positioning and standing. Ease can be created in these difficult situations if you have this basic understanding.

Awakenings

Ivo said, *"Awakenings ignite you. It is indeed possible to be inspired by another's inspiration. Awakenings vary, and how they occur varies. The differences and distinctions are part of any divine occurrence. At the time of your awakening, you had the clear intention of finding a new place. An awakening is affected by one's intention and preparedness. It's not just the effect of one's intention but also the position of one's preparedness. What is sometimes wanted or desired is sometimes satisfied by intention but sometimes not because the preparedness and intention are not aligned. The intention can represent one's willingness to detach. It varies for all.*

Reflections

I had no consciousness awareness of these two requirements.

Cold Hands

My hands started to turn cold as soon as I walked into the room. As I gave Chris Reiki from above the bed, they started to get even colder. In a few minutes, they were freezing. I needed a pair of gloves. Why were they so cold?

Reflections

Ivo said, *"A reversal of energy. Whatever occurs is what needs to occur. Through the process, your client created some release, and it was not appropriate or advisable for you to have absorption. The frigidity was the absence of absorption. It was important for you not to absorb what was being released. What you experienced by the absence of absorption was coldness. There was a force and energy in play that obstructed any absorption to your body and energy. The coldness stopped her release from reaching your body and energy. The release would only occur if she was assured there would be no absorption by you. She identified your sensitivity, and lines of distinction were drawn. Your souls communicated this arrangement. When you walked into the room, you were already cold. You were not warm until you left. As you gave, she absorbed and accepted what was needed. The uniqueness of the treatment was warming to her heart."*

Another soul-to-soul communication on the subconscious level. Our souls worked together so she could absorb Reiki without hurting me. Wonderful healings and releases can occur without our conscious awareness.

Flash of Red

Ivo told me, *"Watch out for a flash of red. He will come to you. Allow your gaze to follow his path. He will lead you and guide you in a particular way. A teacher of sorts. You will know the moment. Let your eyes follow the path. Pay attention. There is a lesson to be learned."*

A beautiful red cardinal flew to the top of a dead tree. I stood and watched carefully. I didn't want to miss anything. The cardinal just sat there. Then a minute later, it flew to another branch. It didn't seem to be in a hurry. The cardinal left the tree and landed on a nearby bush. Again just sitting like it had all the time in the world. Then I heard the word *patience*, and it flew out of sight.

Reflections

That was the message. That was the lesson. I needed to be more patient. I felt a sense of peace come over me. I accepted patience as a valuable tool. Ivo said, *"Each moment is just as significant as the next. Each place is as profound as the one that follows. There is no need to be outside the moment prior to the moment. Be content in the moment. More peace and contentment are available and attainable from this position."*

Sands of Time

My channel said my body turned into an hourglass during our energy work. She said, "You became a beautiful hourglass right before my eyes. The sands of time were moving from the top of your body to the bottom. I had a glimpse of your lifespan. You are not on your last leg. There is more sand on the bottom than the top. I see you living to around ninety years old."

Reflections

Ivo made the hourglass available for my channel and myself. I think he wanted to give me a true perspective on my current life and timeline. I saw myself as having a much-shorter life. It looks like I have more time than I thought.

Out of Body

My channel assisted me on my out-of-body experience. My channel said, "You raised up out of your body. You were hovering and observing. This enabled you to get a good glimpse of yourself. You appeared as a hazy cloud. You wanted to see and observe yourself from the outside. When you finished, you went back into your body."

Reflections

Ivo said, *"This can be done whenever you want, but it mainly happens during sleeping hours."*

Pain

I had a terrible Herxheimer last night, just like old times. Pain, pain, pain. Unrelenting pain. I finally passed out on the bathroom floor. I thought I was finished with Lyme disease! It caught me totally off guard. Was my Lyme back with a vengeance?

Reflections

Ivo said, *"Your recent painful Herx was a bodily remembrance. The Herx gathered your attention and focus, but that was not the heart and core of it all. It's hard for humans to understand. The pain and discomfort were but one spoke of the wheel, not the center. The Herx unearthered grief and sadness, but it was met by your courage and bravery.*

"The Lyme changed everything about you. Your body will never be the same. You see that you are different in other levels, and the physical deserves the same. You acknowledge, embrace, and celebrate the other levels, and the physical deserves the same. One does not come without the other. The Herxing will come and go as it desires. It has nothing to do with the Rife machine or anything else you do. This is part of your process. You are progressing quite nicely. Before you saw no redeeming value in your Herxing. Now you do. It is important for you to know that all is temporary. There should be no attachment or judgment of the Herx. Judgment creates difficulty in acceptance. You are working toward completion and conclusion of this process.

"You are well! Do not turn on yourself when you are in a dark moment. Many use the body in this way. It's very transforming and attention gathering. It requires your focus and dedication. Nothing gathers your attention like pain. The ability to attend to yourself is enhanced when your physical well-being is compromised."

The Herxing grounds me; it brings be down to earth. The pain connects me to those who suffer. I am so grateful when it ends. Pain continues to be part of my process.

Airplane Attachment

I boarded the plane and found an aisle seat in an exit row. I felt fortunate to have such a great seat. I had a lot more room than most people on the plane. Soon a young man slid into the middle seat. We exchanged a few words, and the plane took off. I started to feel uncomfortable sitting next to him, so I went to the back of the plane and felt much better. When I got back to my seat, I started to feel uneasy again, so I defined my space energetically. I pushed my presence outward and said, "This is mine." Soon

I felt even worse. It was bizarre. Why was this young man making me so uncomfortable?

Reflections

Ivo said, *"The young man was traveling with his grandmother's spirit, Phyliss. They were attached. She assigned herself to her grandson. It works for both of them. There was no interest in you until you started defining your space. She perceived that you were doing voodoo. She didn't cotton to your voodoo. She was getting bigger and bigger. She was responding to you, and you were responding to her. She was taking care of her grandson. It escalated. When you went to the back of the plane, the physical distance helped. There was a lot of misperception by both of you. You were both in preservation mode. It was an out-of-the-ordinary event. Very uncommon."*

Ivo continued, *"Energetic energy is very seldom acknowledged or attended to in this world. We acknowledge the physical, mental, and emotional planes but often forget the energetic. The plane incident has masked to you because you did not leave it on the plane. You could have left it on the plane, but you didn't."*

It was true; I still felt uncomfortable about the incident. My channel suggested I say the following to Phyliss: "I honor the love you have for your grandson." I said the words, and the uneasiness vanished. Thank you, Ivo, for your explanation of this strange event. Thank you channel, for helping me remove the discomfort I still carried.

My Mother's Passing

Ivo said, *"She is working her way into the light. She is in transition, acquiring peace."*

Reflections

Ivo said, *"There was an acknowledgment of your mother's passing. You are primarily holding it in your head. More head than heart. Okay, but that's not all there is. We opened the door and reminded you of the access between the head and heart. The relationship was reintroduced to experience the loss in both places. Heart activity is appropriate at some point. It's a choice."*

My Channel and Ivo

My special guest at the book signing was my channel. How lucky was I to see her outside the bookstore? I needed her support. I had been sick for several days and wondered if I could talk without coughing. Her presence gave me strength and peace. I knew my guides were with me. Everything was fine when I walked into the bookstore. The nervousness, jitters, and flulike symptoms disappeared. After the program, I said to her, "It was nice having both of you here." We both smiled and hugged, knowing it was true. The three of us were there. I was so fortunate to have her support and Ivo's presence when I wasn't feeling well.

Reflections

Ivo said, *"You did a fine job at the bookstore, and a good time was had by all. The help you received does not diminish the value of your own contribution."*

Promises

My channel said she felt my promises, conviction, dedication, devotion, and purity. Ivo said, *"They were made prior to your life. Your promises were of soulful origination. Some of the processes will remain soulful, and some will be brought to a physical and human status. That which you intended and promised were part of granting you access to this life's existence. Sometimes several beings are lined up for the same body. Sometimes more than one soul is awaiting the opportunity to enter into that opportunity. One gets it, and others don't. Often it is the best fit, karma, or that which will create the greatest intentions, goals, and accomplishments. It is a matter of finding the best match and proper placement between souls, bodies, and physical experiences. The promises you made are part of what granted you the opportunity."*

Reflections

What promises did you make?

Full Self

Ivo said, *"It's okay for you to be brilliant, flashy, and eye-catching. You do not have to be subdued. You can be vibrant, dynamic, and colorful. You have a tendency to walk on the side of caution. Allow yourself to experience your full self. The best way to help others unfurl is to let others experience your process. Don't let words get in the way. Just be it. You will be more comfortable. Don't straddle the line. Create a pure demonstration of self—your own glorious nature. Be who you are while you are in the presence of others. When you allow others to witness your change, you are giving them permission to acknowledge their own."*

Reflections

Embrace your full self. This will encourage others to do the same.

Brother

My brother suffers from Huntington's disease. I could hear him yelling at the nurse behind the bathroom door. He was upset.

Reflections

Ivo said, *"There's a lot of color around him—a sense of illumination that is demonstrated by his inner essence. This is his confusion. Showing his confusion confirms it more. Sometimes he responds with aggressive behavior and other times he shuts down. He uses two responses at opposite ends of the spectrum. What he is searching for is a release, sometimes exploding, sometimes shutting down. All his color works in his favor. It is better than being gray. He chooses to be colorful. His aura has advantages for him. He has just as much opportunity* as most and more opportunities than some. It was his intention to transverse widely. He has experienced extremes so as to have a full-body experience.

"Whenever one looks at another, it's an outside position. It's not you, and you are not in it. Even when you try to walk in someone else's shoes, it's not possible. It's useful for you and others to honor and embrace the courage of another." I honor and embrace my brother's choices and courage. My brother's soul chose a body with Huntington's disease. That's how it works. I respect divine processes.

Ouch!

I stood on my paddleboard and waited for the wave. I could see the ocean rising up behind me. With two or three strokes, I caught the wave and dropped down the face. The speed was exhilarating. I made a left turn and started heading down the line. What a thrill to roll up and down the face of this beautiful wave. Silky smooth turns; I was in heaven.

Reflections

When I came in, I realized I had a problem. I had a hernia.

Ivo said, *"Don't put your body in a position you may not be ready for. Sometimes an adrenaline flow can mask one's ability to gage one's capability. With the paddleboard injury, the adrenaline masked your recognition of what was too much for you. The thrill of the moment masked your awareness of what overextension might be.*

"It's also a component of your body aging. The body develops wear and tear as it ages. It was not careless. You were in the moment, and the adrenaline created a feeling of being superhuman. These things happen."

After surgery, Ivo said, *"You were bombarded by the anesthesia. Give it a good three weeks from today. Do not push yourself; be gentle and supportive of every aspect of your healing. When you feel good, you need to curtail your activity. The change of your routine has created despair, a wandering and looking for self. Remember that everything you are and have been are within. You just don't feel like yourself. The tricky part is not extending yourself when you feel better. Be with yourself in a kind fashion.*

"The thoroughness of healing is important. The doctor goes by the physical and common. Consider this a time to retreat, to restore and find balance. Your position is slightly askew. That's why you don't feel like yourself. Your relationship to all is different at this time. When your position to yourself changes, your position to all changes."

Tarot Cards

I found myself sitting in front of the tarot card reader. I held the deck of cards as she requested. Then I split the cards into three piles. She took the top three cards off each deck and laid them on the table. They looked like game cards, with people and dragons from the middle ages. She started talking. How could she know so much about me? She told me she hears what to say from the other side. Sometimes spirits show up to deliver messages. She was so accurate.

Reflections

Ivo said, *"Tarot cards are an ancient tool for some to attune to the truth. You were attracted to the energy of the cards. It captured your attention and awareness. You were comfortable with her."*

Movie

The movie theater was fairly empty. As my wife and I watched the movie, I noticed I was downloading light. I was giving myself Reiki. My hands were warm, and the flow was very strong. It's hard to believe self-Reiki is possible in such a noisy environment, but it worked and I felt energized after the movie.

Reflections

Ivo said, *"There was a true and real pause that was created by the movie. You chose to respond to your need and desire for treatment. Your need prompted the offering. You were very aware of yourself. You willingly provided for that need. The movie was a simple and singular occupation. It helped that the theater was not crowded. Everyone was focused on the movie, and there was very little distraction. The movie did not over-engage you. It was a safe environment."* Divine light is always available!

Monarch Butterfly

This morning I saw a beautiful monarch butterfly. Then I heard the words, "You are exactly the same."

Reflections

Ivo said, *"The butterfly was attracted by your light. When you are in nature, you almost always release you defenses. You become more pure. Nature makes you feel safer. An exchange with the butterfly was possible because of the safety you felt."*

We are all one. We are not separate. Oneness is a wonderful feeling.

Memorial Service

It was a picture-perfect day. Colorado blue sky, puffy white clouds, a small pond with geese. A gentle breeze carried cottonwood seeds into the air. It seemed to be snowing on a beautiful, sunny day in May. Chris loved to ski. Most of the people here had skied with her. The white snowflakes continued to land on our shoulders and the tops of our heads. They drifted into the pond and surrounded us with God's love.

When the formal service concluded, we all walked to the top of a small hill. Everyone received a balloon. One, two, three, and they were released in unison—white balloons rising in a perfect harmony. Within a few moments, a large white crane started circling above our heads. Everyone pointed to the bird. Do you see the bird? Is that Chris? Is she saying goodbye to us? Our hearts were lightened; they were filled with wonder and joy.

Reflections

Ivo said, *"Chris was honored by the level of love and willingness to pay tribute to her life. It gave people what they needed. The bird was sent to bring comfort."*

Acquaintance

I recently met a young man who made me feel uncomfortable. Why?

Reflections

Ivo said, *"You felt his imbalance. You were uncomfortable with his carelessness. Some would say he was a lost soul. He was walking aside of his path. He was at the edge of what was okay for him. The soul had intentions for him, which he was not abiding by. If he continues, he will have a wake-up call. Everything he does at this time is in combat with his father. He's upset at his father. He is not getting what he needs from his dad. He never felt secure, safe, or stable with his father. He is straddling the line. It's all up to him."*

When one feels uncomfortable with another, there is often a reason. Trust your intuition, and act appropriately.

Picabo

Our cat, Picabo, is getting older. She's had a few accidents in the house.

Reflections

Ivo said, *"They represent her response to losing control in her life and world. The accidents demonstrate her control. These processes are occurring within her growth patterns. If you use your position of power, it will get worse. You can try giving her things to be in control of. She needs to feel in control, safe, and in charge. Try to communicate with her that she is safe. Don't physically come down on her. Just pull your energy back when she does something undesirable. Dogs are more trainable. Cats are unpredictable. Dogs are black and white. Cats can be very challenging. They are an elusive species."*

Things are now wonderful with Picabo. No more accidents.

Capacity

Ivo said, *"There was a winding up of energy. Your heart expanded, and there was a cleansing and purification. Strength and capacity were increased, along with your standing. This process increased what you can hold energetically. Your capacity for energy was increased, more volume than weight. Vibration would be more of a weight. It gives you the opportunity to be more purely and clearly occupied by you and to be more comfortable within your own."*

Reflections

My capacity to hold energy increased during my last energy session. This is a good thing. I can now offer more to others. As Ivo said, *"Don't dilute yourself by reducing your own energy, by setting some of your own energy outside, or by allowing others' energy to come within you."*

Disciple of Truth

Ivo said, *"You are a disciple of truth, a follower of truth, and a follower of the divine. You are led by an interest in being devoted to **all**—nothing external or outside. It is not a mindful awareness or intention but a resonance of you with all that exists. We are all divine. We are all in a divine existence. There is something powerful about devotion not being limited to one thing or* *individual. If you focus on the individual, you lose the whole. The individual can be distracting. Truth is not oriented from partial reference. Truth can be found there, but it is not limited to that or what can be absorbed."*

Reflections

Truth works for me.

Outer Body Experiences

Ivo said, *"When you no longer need the safety and security of the body, you can experience things outside the body. It is a method of expansion. When you go into a sleeping state, you freely relinquish the soul. This gives you an opportunity to sense and experience your life in a broader way. More awareness is available. Out, in, out, in, very playful. It is part of your process and development. Outer body experiences are optional for you. You have already begun to experience this process. To see more broadly and less conclusively. It has become part of your process. This contributes to your empathy. You are comfortable doing this. The releasing of your soul opens the door for extension beyond human parameters. The holding of self, soul, spirit, and essence are not locked. There are extensions to this process that you have yet to experience."*

Reflections

Great.

9-11

Ivo said, *"9-11 was a monumental event—a horrific event. It changed so many people and things. A majority of people on earth were focused on it at the same time. After 9-11, the majority of people on earth, greater than half, which is an incredible number, shared consciousness. That is profound. Over half were thinking about the same thing at the same moment. They were attuned to the same thing, a shared focus. A new consciousness was created. It enhanced the possibilities of the world. Remember, there is always a bigger picture. What appears to be is not only what is. Remember, karma is always balancing. It changed so many people and things. There is always justice and balance. It is not something one can expect the human mind and heart to accept."*

Reflections

Good things can come out of bad things, but it is often difficult to accept from a human perspective.

Unknown Commodity

Ivo said, *"Look at yourself as an unknown commodity. Give yourself the opportunity to experience more of what you want and need to experience in your lifetime and body. Patterns and routines can reflect who you have become, not just what you have been. Don't assume you know your position. What you want, need, and desire now may be different as compared to the past, or who you are now and who you have become!"*

Reflections

We are all works in progress.

Prediction

Ivo said, *"A young lady in her twenties will come into your life. There's a childlike aspect with her. It's an opportunity for her to get something from you that she did not get from her father. It is more about her than you. Something that she is without. Something that she can get from knowing you. This will happen within eight months. Don't assume a parental role. She needs to find that parental role elsewhere.*

There is also some past life history between you. She was torn out of your arms. It was quite traumatic for both of you at that time. She was a boy at the time in his teens and was taken from you. Some societies did this in the past. It was slavery. Most strong feelings that we have are preregistered. They come from someplace else, a previous life, something captured and demonstrated before. The soul knows! Each of you enjoyed the reminder. It is like running into someone you haven't seen in a long time. You have a history together."

Reflections

I met the young lady, and there was a special bond between us. Our souls were happy to see each other. I did not mention our past life connection. Not everyone is ready for such a conversation. Maybe when she gets older. In the meantime, our friendship continues to grow.

Brother's Departure

Ivo said, *"His soul is considering departure. He's looking for a way out—any way or place. he's skirting the perimeter to find a way out, to escape. It will be an illness. He wants you to know it is his choice. He is figuring it out. it will be nothing immediate. He is in the process of considering and negotiating. Everyone's process is distinct and unique as the individual. Each has their own method of passage. Remember, it is what he has chosen. He's coming to a new place, position, and change. It's very natural. He's on a cusp of a change and transformation. It's appropriate for him, and it's exactly where he needs to be and to be doing at the moment. Feeling guilty does not celebrate your choices or his."*

Reflections

My brother's departure is between his soul and God. Ivo's words gave me a new perspective and eased my pain.

Dignity

Ivo said, *"A small amount of dignity was released from your core. Waves of energy came out of your center. Remember, we each have our essence. When you shift, churn, extend, and expand, those changes are taken with you. Your change affects and influences all. Everything you are contributes to everything that is. Everything that is, is affected by your change and transformation. It's not to be measured. Do not discount or diminish the significance of events like this that happen to people all the time everywhere."*

Reflections

These events happen all the time to everyone. What you do matters, and it affects our world and all that is.

Stressors

Ivo said, *"There's a wide prospect of stressors out there that your body experiences and feels. Anything that changes in your life can be a stressor. It is about identifying them and responding consciously and supportively. Stress is another word for imbalance. Utilize your sensitivity effectively. View your sensitivity as supportive, not restrictive. You can use it to be more aware. Make adjustments for yourself. You may become intolerant of the imbalances. This is a favorable progression. It can be inconvenient and uncomfortable, but it is preferred because you will experience less stress in your life. The pace of progression varies from person to person, but everyone is progressing. Human living comes with stressors. You get to choose your position in how you respond."*

Reflections

Identify the stressors in your life, and try to minimize them. Make adjustments to avoid unnecessary pain and suffering.

Kissed by a Tree

The tree is located on a path to the Nosara Yoga Institute in Costa Rica. It is magnificent. I could feel its beauty, strength, and wisdom as I approached. I placed my hands on its silky-smooth trunk, and they started to pulse. I grounded myself deep into the earth. My chest started to expand as I asked for restoration. After a few minutes, I stepped away from the tree. That was a powerful experience!

Reflections

Ivo said, *"It is an old wise tree that has experienced much. Its wisdom is well earned. The tree is father to many, plants, animals, trees, and people. The tree is 183 years old. Many have come and gone throughout its lifetime. You sensed that the tree was alive. It was appreciative of your admiration and glances that you gave it physically and within yourself. It gave you a broader awareness of the tree and what it offers and brings. It enjoyed being seen by you because you were very thorough in your experience of it. Life is the nature of existence. A tree does not attempt to be human. Trees have essence. Your heart was kissed by the tree. It was an expression of affection and love. You were ready for it. A kiss is a connection and union. You are a tree hugger and kisser. Many have been kissed by a tree, but few will recognize it or be able to express it. The tree and you will always be part of one another forevermore. There is a tangible distinction that you will well remember. This was profound and will stay with you always."* I wear a ring that commemorates this special moment.

Play for Your Own Team

Ivo said, *"You are experiencing your resiliency more consistently. It feels more normal and reliable to you. You are willing to make considerations and concessions more freely than you have in the past. You are gentler with yourself than you were in the past. Give yourself the opportunity to stay the course. There is more consideration and less judgment now. You are beginning to play for your own team. You are turning the tide, no space or holes in it. So much of it is your belief that it is so. It doesn't have to be comprehended by you to be accepted. You have come to a position where you are more resilient."*

Reflections

We all need to play for our own team, be our own best friends. When we honor ourselves, we honor God.

Leaving the Florida Lyme Disease Association

Ivo said, "*The e-mail responses gave concrete clarity for leaving in case you were in doubt. The timing was perfect. The release of focus and responsibility will act a vacuum to invite more. In the interim it is okay to rest. Learn to live without it and settle into that comfortably. There's a proper amount of restoration that needs to occur so the energy of invitation develops. It is a wait and see, not a scavenger hunt. There is no lack of areas that could utilize your services. There were no missed opportunities. You gained a lot of useful knowledge. It was some of your best work. Remember to always regard your contribution as a success. You were successful in the fruition of your intention. Be rightfully proud.*"

Reflections

Thank you, Ivo, for your kind words. I cofounded the Northeast Florida Lyme Association in 2009, which later became the Florida Lyme Disease Association. I resigned from the Florida Lyme Disease Board in 2014.

Car Accident

Ivo said, "*You were a willing participate in the car accident, but it had more to do with the other driver. What occurred had a ripple effect. It's the hope and intention that the other driver will grow and learn, but it is unsure at the moment. There's an opportunity for change and transformation with him. Maybe. The more painful something is in the short-term, or the long-term, the greater the results. The accident or incident was not a mistake or out of order. More truthful to use the term incident participation. The car accident was a planned event, determined prior by a couple of days. You made yourself available for that type of participation. These can be planned, determined prior, or instantaneous. The driver of the other car may have short- and long-term changes as a result of the accident. The changes can become permanent, but old habits die hard. Fear, laziness, and lack of trust in self can send one back to previous habits. It is unclear at this time how it is going to play out."*

Reflections

This was an eye-opener for me. My jeep rolled three times because my soul volunteered to possibly assist a young man. How much of the human experience is really in our conscious hands? What deals and agreements are being made by your soul? Another eye-opener for me!

Egg Hatching

Ivo said, *"Today was an egg-hatching day for you. Many were present. A rippling flow of energy occurred. A cap on stress was released, physically, emotionally, soulfully, and energetically. This will broaden and manage your manner. Respond generously to yourself. Think of stress as an imbalance. Identify stress, and attend to it. No more sensitivity is needed, but use it wisely. You are intolerant of ignoring yourself now. A higher learning capacity has taken place. A seed of consciousness has been planted. A willingness to allow shifts and changes is being supported. Everything that you are contributes to everything that is. Everything that is, is affected by your transformation."*

Reflections

A seed of consciousness was planted.

Mexican Hat Utah

Ivo said, *"It is an energetic portal. You sensed, felt, and experienced it. It's a physical location where energy can be increased due to power plays or positions. The intensity of energy can be greater. In and out. It's a door. You had a physical sensation of the different energy. Some portals are used, some have been used, some are dormant, and some will be used. Mexican Hat is not a place you need to be to serve others."*

Dane Boggs

Reflections

I did not feel comfortable in the area.

Moab Utah

Ivo said, *"You are in sync with the vibration there. It is a higher vibration. It feels like home, not a portal. You can be at ease there. It doesn't require anything of you to be there. You are attuned to it. There is a resonation that is reflective of you and you of it. It is a place to be utilized for respite and restoration. You do not need to be there. It's a nice place to visit, not your place to be."*

Reflections

This explains why I went there to beat Lyme disease and why I have taken so many trips to the area. It's my vibrational oasis in the desert.

Tiger Moth

Ivo said, *"The tiger moth in Sedona was a dance of energies. It was having fun as well. The life span is only a couple of months in that phase. You were wowed by it. You were entranced by it. The first time you see something new in nature, it is extra special. Purity was present."*

Reflections

I couldn't take my eyes off the Tiger Moth. It was so beautiful.

Nature

Ivo said, *"You have a very strong sense of the divine and the purity of nature, as a human and spiritual being. It's a combined experience, which is not uncommon for you. It's one of the reasons you seek nature, a recurring theme. It is very resourceful for you. It gives you interest and willingness to carry on."*

Reflections

The purity of nature refreshes my soul. Does it do the same for you?

Mortimer

Ivo said, *"Mortimer was here to support you in garnering knowledge—your absolute sense of knowing. An opportunity is coming soon where some learning is available. He is your tutor. It will be three to six months from now. It is a pretty formal process, opening up what you have and what you know."*

Reflections

More divine help and assistance. We all have assistance that is appropriate for our paths.

Mirabai Devi

Ivo said, *"Your encounter with her allowed you to celebrate your differences. To each his own. To each her own, to each his own. It gave you the opportunity to sense, feel, and experience who you are and your investment in that. You are invested in yourself and who you are. It was a meet-and-greet surface event. You realized that you do not want to be her. You identified more with your own than hers, which is profound. By all appearances, you would share something, but there were more differences than similarities."*

Reflections

I am so glad I had the opportunity to meet her one on one. Mirabai brings love and light to the world. She is a true blessing!

Dane Boggs

Reiki Treatments

Ivo said, *"Reiki is God light and God energy. There is a giver and receiver. Both parts are of equal significance. It goes beyond what is just appropriate and inappropriate. There are all kinds of dynamics that affect, influence, and temper the offering. They cannot interfere with the work, but everyone is not in the same place or able to receive in the same way. Willingness, fear, hesitation—these can change what occurs. What happens is affected by what is offered and received, the connection between you and them and their position. There are so many variances, but it is all perfect. There are infinite variances of light and doorways. Typically such an exchange is agreed upon prior. When you work with another, it is important to garner his or her permission."*

Reflections

Reiki is so complex and yet so simple at the same time. I focus on transferring as much light as possible, knowing it will go where it is most needed. Any healing that takes place is between them and the divine. Healing will not occur unless it is appropriate for them at that time and place.

Liftoff

Ivo said, *"You are preparing for liftoff before the end of the year. Changing your position and altering your association with this world is a type of progression. Your destination shall be reached by the end of the year. It is primarily spiritual, but it does have physical ramifications. Docking has a tendency to take more time and energy. Docking does not always take place prior to liftoff. You are fueling up for liftoff. It is a journey for those who have an interest in growth and are prepared. You will soon be ready and able for the production. The liftoff is coming between November 21, 2014 and November 23, 2014. The dates can shift. It is set up for those dates. It's generated by your change in vibration. You will feel the difference."*

Reflections

Ivo said, *"It happened on November 22, 2014, and yes it was successful. The postscript was February 13, 2015. What you wanted to accomplish occurred. The density and compatibility of your neurons changed. It was complete or near to complete in November, but something in February concluded the process."* It was part of my path as per Ivo.

Mars

Ivo said, *"Yes, there is a form of life on Mars that is not recognizable by humans. At one time Mars was more earthlike than earth. Mars has shared commonalities and vast differences with earth. It has its own inhabitants. We would perceive it as a new form of life. At this point, there is very little that we can understand. It cannot be perceived from a human vantage point due to our limited perceptions and limited awareness around life and what constitutes life."*

Reflections

Look for a different form of life on Mars.

Grounding

Ivo said, *"Your presence and position on earth need to be grounded. It remains necessary and important. As you grow and evolve your sensitivity requires grounding. Different methods and intentions will be required. It needs to be consistently adjusted and different. What you did in the past will not work as it once did. As long as you are in the physical body, you must be dedicated to grounding. Grounding increases your vibration without fear of departure. It does not work this way for everyone, but it does for you. The ability to extend and expand soulfully is often supported and encouraged when you feel secure. You tend to extend more when you are secure in the connection between body and soul. Less than half are interested in extending and expansion at your level. Continue to ground yourself. Conscious intention is important."*

Reflections

Grounding is important for me, and I practice it different ways during the day. Just saying the word *earth* can make a huge difference in how I feel. When I say the word, I feel connected to the center of the planet.

Egan

During the energy work, Egan said, "That's my boy!" Ivo said, *"It was a proud father moment. A real sense of paternal energy was conveyed on the same capacity as your father. Don't think about it much. All is one. All is one, so he is your father and Egan at the same time. The personal self and the whole are not separate. We are not separate from all. Our higher self does not fit into the body. Egan and your dad in this lifetime are one and the same. It doesn't make sense from a human perspective."* My channel said, "You were not ready to hear this till now. It is not that far-fetched. It may be new to you, but it is not extraordinary."

Reflections

It is hard to grasp and accept but true since we are all one!

Zapped

Ivo said, *"You got zapped during your Qi-Gong practice. A bolt of energy entered your body from the sky. You were in nature, and you were seeking that which raises your vibration. Your resonation with nature and your recognition and connection to all made this possible. Your vibration reached a level where you got zapped, where you felt and knew all. A suspension occurred. You were not attached to the human standing. You were not held to the body. This was a suspension. it was not an out-of-body experience, which is a journey elsewhere. You stayed where you were. You had a moment where you felt the whole of you and the whole of all. You were absolutely there. You lost that sense of gravity, of being one. You sensed, knew, and experienced you as part of all that is, knowing oneness. You enjoyed the suspension."*

Reflections

It was a magical experience for me.

Message

Prior to a Reiki treatment, I heard, *"She does not have a headache!"* Ivo said, *"The message you received was correct. She has a true detachment and disconnect from her body—not a soulful detachment but emotional and psychological. She does not like her body at this time. This can create mis-associations with it and miscalculations. There is a disconnect between her and her body. She could benefit most by avoiding self-loathing. You can't do it for her. It's a learning process for you and her. Just be who you are. Setting an example is a big part of it. Show her how else it can be done. She's very critical of herself in many ways. Try not to let her get away with it. Call her on it. Give her an opportunity to know there is an option."*

Reflections

I did the best I could as instructed by Ivo.

Status Update

Ivo said, *"You have one foot in the spiritual world and one in the physical world. Intention does more than anything else. Your steadiness and ability to position yourself evenly in this world was stated by Egan. Do not allow yourself to feel upset when the outcome and intention are not the same, because most of the time they are. You are consistently creating and supporting balance within yourself. The more you grow and evolve, the greater your sensitivity, and the more likely you are to feel the presence of balance and imbalance. A sensitive person may sense an imbalance that is very slight. Don't regard the imbalance as monumental. You have more balance than ever before. You have created a position for yourself at this time that is beyond any position you have held in the physical body so far—beyond any human incarnation of the past. Keep in mind that movement forward, which is progression, is the human experience for each of us. All of us are moving in a direction that is more than we were before.*

The vibration of all on earth is greater than in the past. As a people, we are in an advanced state of being. Everything that occurs in this world at this time is part of a passage from the past to the future. It is the intention of this world and these people to bring that which has been at a certain level and standing to a place and position that is beyond where it has been before. This has been attained, but there is more to go. The advancement of humankind as we know it is unfurling very quickly. It's one of the reasons why there feels like an intensity that is gathering here on earth. Now what was obtained in three to four lifetimes can be obtained in half a lifetime. The blending of energies is much different than ever before. There is much more collective energy being exuded.

It is your part to be perceived as enough where you create your offering and your contribution in the purest passing possible. Recognize your strength and standing. You have developed a willingness to participate in whatever way you might be guided, divined, or invited to participate. It used to have to be logical, have a reason, make sense, or be familiar. Now you have a willingness to let God show you what you can be used for. You recognize that you come to know more by your willingness to participate without parameters. Your need to understand in the past was limiting. You have set that aside. You trust the world. It's a progressive position that leaves you with spare energy. You no longer need to make sense of everything."

Reflections

We are all moving forward toward a higher planetary consciousness. I have trust and faith in the future of humankind. There is so much help on the other side for each and every one of us. When bad things happen, remember that good things normally follow in larger amounts.

Mother

My deceased mother is being well attended to. Ivo said, *"Her interest is in taking it slowly. Being well tended is comforting to her. She likes being able to determine her own pace. She appreciates this. It's a transitional phase. The review is not likely to be taken lightly. Multiple ancestors and guides are helping. Having all the time in the world helps. She is doing it all in her own way and her own time. She recognizes the passing was well worth the wait. Prior to that time, she thought she was ready at one point, long before the passage went down, and now recognizes the benefit of her particular passage."*

Reflections

It is nice to know she is being well cared for on the other side. The review process is something we all do after departure.

Big Tree in Guana State Park

Ivo said, *"It is 152 years old and welcomes you. You like it because it greets you. It says, 'Come on in.'"*

Reflections

I love that tree!

Broken Dishes

We broke two dishes and one wine glass at our house during a recent birthday party. It all happened at once while we were cutting the cake. Ivo said, *"A son who passed on recently was awkward in making his presence known. He is not agile in his conveyance. It was not intentional. Some are better than others."*

Reflections

This makes you wonder about the things that happen each day.

Keys

I recently locked my keys inside the car. A vision occurred moments before it actually happened. I stood outside my care absorbing the shock and wonder. Ivo said, *"Typically those kinds of signs and symbols are faint. More than common awareness made the circumstance not as disappointing. Excitement took away some of the disappointment. Listen closely, and there is a different feeling between watching it happen or imagining it happening. Watching is an awareness, and sometimes you can change the outcome and sometimes not. Discern and tell the difference. Imagining puts energy into motion that looks a particular way. Watching is being an observer. Sometimes you are just a watcher."*

Reflections

I caught myself watching the future unfold but was unable to change the outcome.

Karmic Debt

My wife and I recently helped a young lady settle into our community. Ivo said, *"A karmic debt was cleared for both of you. It's almost impossible to avoid collecting karmic debt. It's part of living. Being earnest in the resolve of debt removal is very important. Being true and interested in making amends is necessary for debt removal. Having difficulties and resolving them for yourself is how you conclude and complete the history. It's how you bring things back to balance again. In your case, you were one of three male students at a boarding school. There was an unsettled dynamic between the three of you. Much of it being personality conflicts, high jinks, pranks, and jokes. The three of you had things to learn and do differently, and this provided the opportunity to conclude that history. That's how it works."*

Reflections

Less karmic debt is a good thing. As Ivo said, *"This realization can make you less invested in your pain."*

Path

My channel said, "We are all on our path. How could it be otherwise? Wherever you are, you are on your path. It belongs to you."

Reflections

We each have our unique paths.

Catch

I looked out the window and saw Catch in the driveway with our cat, Noire. They do enjoy each other's company. It's a pretty cool experience for myself and anyone passing the house. A yellow lab and black cat hanging out together as buddies!

Reflections

Ivo said, *"Moments like that allow us to feel and know the beauty and perfection of this existence. It's a simple pleasure. Recognize as many as you can as often as you can."*

Offerings

Ivo said, *"When making your offerings, remember, they are often feeling sick and powerless. They are victims to a large extent. Give them some power. When you request their permission, you are giving them power. Garner their approval first. You might say, "I have information that might be of interest to you. If you want to talk, please give me a call sometime." This approach will be respectful of their position. Leave them with a gift of power!"*

Reflections

That was good advice for me.

Alan

My channel said, "A new guide named Alan was present with Egan. They were interacting with a fluid, silvery white light. It ran from your crown chakra to your heart and solar plexus. The solar plexus rooted and tied off the energy. Alan is the punctuater. He brings in what is needed. You have made changes, so where you go and what you are, are influenced by this shift in your heart. A transformation has occurred where you can convey and carry that kind of energy in a clear, concise, and consistent capacity. There's a responsibility that comes with that so you can now be more deliberate in bringing yourself to the world."

Reflections

Ivo said, *"Your heart is holding its own at this time in a very pure capacity. The energy of you exudes more purely of love than it has before. You are broadening your heart energy. It is becoming a natural habit for you. It's usable and effective."* Wonderful.

Aerial Beings

Ivo said, *"Aerial Beings are working to stir the energy around you to support within and outside your transformation. Most of the effect is external—life, world, where you go, and what you do."*

Reflections

Thank you.

Brother's Departure

Ivo said, *"There is a shift that he has created because he is tired. Vitality has diminished, and exhaustion has set in with it. It is very challenging to be strong, vital, and complete. It's helpful for you to know. He's not giving up, but there is a point where the essence of one can get fatigued to a level where the effort is* too much and too hard. *His processes are his processes. His courage deserves a great deal of respect on a human being level and soul level. Honor and respect him for the choices he has made.*"

Reflections

Ivo's words have helped me see and understand the shifting that has occurred. I honor and respect his courage and the choices he has made for departure.

Stephanie

Ivo said, "*It was an instantaneous connection—a sense and feel of a connection like no other. For you it was like meeting one of your own! You gravitate toward them. You can talk to them. There is a similarity between your soul's growth, placement, and advancement. You have taken the same classes between lifetimes. She is of high caliber!*"

Reflections

Magical connections are no accidents.

Self-Help

After the energy session, Ivo said, "*You wanted to do the work yourself. You wanted to use what you had learned. You released pain from your right leg. You participated in a way today that is very uncommon, in your favor. You supported your own progression. It was sometimes conscious and sometimes not. Because of your sensitivity, you may have felt way out of balance but really only slightly askew. The more evolved and attuned you become to your sense of balance, the less tolerant you are of imbalance. It has more to do with your awareness than your actual positioning.*"

Reflections

It is nice to know this is possible for myself and others.

Mother

My channel said, "When I put my hands over your heart, I felt the presence of your mother. The soul connection was acknowledged, and the heart connection was beyond humanness, much more than one can feel in the physical body. You were resonating at the same level and vibration simultaneously. With everything there is a time."

Reflections

So many wonderful things can happen during energy treatments.

Current Status

Ivo said, *"You have chosen a beacon position. You invite and draw others to you. You willingly act as a beacon for those who are interested in experiencing and knowing more. You act as a teacher for others. You have elevated yourself in your evolutionary development and status. You cannot unlearn. If you visit your past with your new self, you create elevation by way of seeing and doing it differently. Circumstances like that can change your growth dramatically. Taking the new you and doing something that you had done before in a different way changes and alters your evolutionary position in a way that is notable."*

Reflections

As per Ivo.

Old Buddy

I asked my channel if my buddy and I had any past life connections. He and I get along so well, it's as if we have known each forever. My Channel said, "I see the two of you rowing together, a big boat, below deck. You are side by side rowing. I see the unison and rhythmic energy of rowing on the port side behind the middle." This seemed to take our relationship back to the Greek or Roman times when such boats existed.

Reflections

It's nice to get verification of past life associations and the strong feelings that often come with them.

Night Sky

Ivo said, *"You are being drawn to the night sky. You have permission to go for it. There is something going on out there that is more profound than before. You begin to sense that. You have nothing to do. Just allow the experience to happen. There is more than what you might fathom or that meets the eye. Give yourself the opportunity to go with it without more understanding. It is already occurring and ongoing. It concerns interplanetary capacity, a well to draw upon. Just experience what you experience."*

Reflections

This has been a pleasurable experience.

Caretaker

Ivo said, *"You have been overusing and abusing your body. There was a time where that was okay. Not now. As a caretaker, that is not okay. Pushing you beyond your balance is borderline stuff. It could have become a deep dark place. It didn't, a few shadows here and there. So much is honoring and respecting yourself. It is within your charge. You are in charge of it, this gift we are given.*

Most of us think of ourselves as caretakers of others, before we take care of ourselves.*"*

Reflections

It all starts with taking care of yourself. This is not an easy thing to do on planet Earth. Be a caretaker to yourself first and foremost.

Museum of Fine Arts, St. Petersburg

When I walked into the Museum of Fine Arts in St. Petersburg, I felt like a ton of bricks had just fallen on me. Why? Ivo said, *"Some had to do with the history of the art. The room was loaded with a lot of energy. Some of the energy was historical. Most caretakers of that kind of facility disperse and distribute the artifacts among the museum. It was congregated in one place being heavier and more impactful for you. Spirits and energy were both in the room. The artifacts have been touched by many hearts and hands, and you experienced the collective energy of both."*

Reflections

It was not a pleasant experience, and now I know why. I had to define my space energetically to feel more comfortable.

Existence

Ivo said, *"Growth and evolvement often occur while we are here on earth, sometimes while we are in the physical body and sometimes while we are no longer in the physical body. Transformation always occurs. It is not something the human mind can typically comprehend, because the mind has a limited capacity. The mind is a conceptual mind. Existence is not a concept."*

Reflections

The human mind has limitations. Acceptance can bring greater peace.

Supporting All

Ivo said, *"No matter how valuable and independent the growth of the individual is, it means nothing without the growth of all. It's not about climbing to the top of the mountain and making it first. It's about staying at the bottom of the mountain and helping everyone else. Independent growth and development are important, but it means nothing without supporting all. It's about wholeness. It's about oneness!"*

Reflections

We are not separate. We are all one. Helping others up the ladder promotes personal growth and good karma. Supporting all connects us to our wholeness and oneness.

Out of Sorts

Ivo said, *"When you feel 'out of sorts' in a small manner or large, it is simply an indication that what you are doing is not working for you. Take a look at the bigger picture, and see where you belong. Choose a place that is comfortable for you because it is appropriate, not a place that is comfortable because it is familiar.*

"Do not be afraid of the swing of emotions that may be experienced. Your human self is full of such emotions. They will find a way out, as you further your process, whether it is comfortable or not. Allow the expanse of feelings to be a release for you. Good riddance. In depth emotions are often carried for years upon years. To feel them is to release them. This release can only further the strength of your standing. Remember to always honor, trust, and follow your heart.

"The greater good brings opportunities for more growth and development. Have awareness of where these opportunities lie. Know your place, and find a way to live there comfortably."

Reflections

Make changes when you are feeling out of sorts. Choose comfort because it is appropriate, not familiar. Letting go of emotions in an appropriate manner is better than carrying them in the body.

Sabu and Watu

Ivo said, *"They came to give you a massage—two huge guys with lightness, gentleness, and playfulness. They are gentle giants. They are here for the new year. They are here to support your process and processes in 2016."*

Reflections

Lucky me.

Matador

Ivo said, *"In another life you were a matador. From that life, you learned not to turn my back on anything that was menacing, like a spike or horn. It originated there. Keep your eye on the ball or bull. You had a real flair, a dramatic flair to performing. Lifetime number fourteen in South America. The body you have now is not much different. You have a similar body carriage."*

Reflections

How many different lives have you had? In my most recent life, I was a crop-dusting pilot and died in an accident. That happened in the 1920s.

I then came back in 1953 for life twenty-eight. This information was provided by Ivo and my channel.

Muscle Testing 1

I recently acquired the ability to muscle test others remotely. No one needs to come to my office. I use a pendulum to get yes and no answers for myself and clients. This becomes their Rife protocol for getting well. Ivo said, *"Your sense of knowing is clarified by this tool. Know that the life of all flows through you and the pendulum carries that forth. You are a divine being and in your own right carry the light of God within. How you use this tool supports the governing station of all eternity. It's a great tool for self-support. Ask permission when muscle testing others. You are extending and strengthening your energy processes and attuning to all at a new level. No attachment to outcome is best. Not working is also okay. Attachment is more likely to interfere."*

Reflections

It is nice to have this new tool for myself and others. Muscle testing can be used for many different situations and circumstances. For example, I often ask the body of my clients what it desires to run on the Rife machine. This provides my clients with specific frequencies and auto channels for each day of the week, reducing the time to make improvements. Muscle testing once a month permits one to make adjustments and changes as per the body's desire. Thank you, All That Is.

Fear and Sadness

I thought about the fear and sadness of Huntington's disease in my life and family. Ivo said, *"Do not disregard fear and sadness. Be with it. Feel it. It can be intense or passive. This prevents shackling so they aren't stored in the body. Release when appropriate."*

Reflection

Thank you.

Your Whole Self

Ivo said, *"Be your whole self while living life. Allow the heart to be open. Find people and situations that are advantageous to you. Share who you are and what you possess with many. Go for it. It is okay. Feeling vulnerable has more to do with that kind of opening and frequency rather than a bad place. Be your whole full self. Validate your own. Grant yourself permission Extend and expand in your fullest capacity. Get behind yourself. It is a natural process. A sense of power and pleasure can occur for you. It can give you a rush, a thrill. You feel charged up, not fatigued. Align yourself in the moment, and a resonation and illumination occur at higher levels."*

Reflections

Let your whole self be seen and witnessed by others.

Coffee Shop

On a recent trip to Salt Lake City, we stopped a coffee shop. The space seemed so familiar. Ivo said, *"Yes, it is the place where you purchased Wayne Dyer's book,* Your Erroneous Zones *in college. The bookstore has changed hands. At that time, the energy of you and the book resonated with one another. The choosing was yours because of the magnetic quality of the book's energy. It was like striking a match. Lots of self-discipline was required to manifest your changes. It would have been unnatural to walk away from the book."*

Reflections

Wayne Dyer's book *Your Erroneous Zones* gave me the opportunity to control my thought patterns, which gave me a new perspective on life. I recommend it to everyone. It was a huge book at just the right time for me. Being able to control one's thoughts, feelings, and emotions is so important. It all comes down to your thoughts. Inner peace starts with loving thoughts for yourself and others. It is not an easy task but possible with practice.

Theresa Caputo

I enjoyed seeing Theresa Caputo as a medium in Florida. She's so wonderful and entertaining as she moves through the audience. At one point during her presentation, I felt very cold and started to shiver. I suspected a presence. Later Ivo said, *"A deceased boyfriend or ex-husband was near you. You felt and sensed him. That was the sensation. It was about him and the lady in front of you. The energy was strong and profound, like someone shouting in a quiet room. That's what you felt. Theresa has a filter that is innately in place. Otherwise she would experience bombardment. It is interesting for you because of the way she tells it. The basic truths are evident for you."*

Reflections

Theresa provides wonderful healing. Thank you, Theresa.

Isolation

Ivo said, *"Isolation for you is enjoyable, but you would not feel that you are providing the greatest benefit for all if you maintained isolation. It is learning how to attend and take care of yourself so you can be in the world. It's not about stepping out of this world."*

Reflections

I do want to make a contribution to All That Is. This requires that I stay as balanced, centered, grounded, and healthy as possible.

Dane Boggs

Herxing

I recently had another painful Herxheimer. Why do I still get them? Ivo said, *"Take good care, my friend, and know all is well. You are a courageous sort who has chosen a path of both presence and remembrance. The two are ingrained in such a way where it can sometimes be difficult to determine the difference. It does not matter. What you need to get, you do. You are a willing soul who uses all he has within his grasp to create personal growth while supporting others in their process of growth as well. Be here now, and know you are loved, supported, and appreciated."*

Reflections

Curling up in a ball of intense pain for hours is a horrible experience. When the pain subsides, I feel so blessed. As Ivo said, *"They are part of your path and processes. You are beginning to see value in them."*

Grounding

Ivo said, *"It is very important for you to consider grounding as a significant aspect of your overall balance, and it can secure you in this world like nothing else. Being here in your fullest capacity, being here and being all you can be, and being as present as you can be. This allows the spiritual human aspect of you to act as one in this earth place. It is a large piece of the puzzle."*

Reflections

Grounding techniques and exercises are very important for my health and well-being.

Sherwin

Ivo said, *"You have overextended and overexerted yourself lately. This makes being here less appealing. It can deny the strong, secure, solid, earthly position you hold. Sherwin showed up. He helped with the dispersing of energy that had occurred. Those extensions were brought back to the center of you little by little. Be aware of any tendency to overextend. You can do simple exercises. Say as you did when a child, 'All lee all ox in free.' Let this bring you back to your center energetically. Call yourself home with this technique."*

Reflections

This is a fun exercise, and it works immediately. It helps me when my energy is scattered, and I want to feel more centered and grounded. Try it! Say the words, *"All lee all ox in free,"* and feel the difference.

Suffering

Ivo said, *"You want to be very conscious of how you perceive or experience another's life. What's suffering for you may not be for them and vice versa. You are aware of a lot of suffering. Be careful what you perceive as suffering for others. Recognize the difference. Sometimes a lack of acceptance will create this perception. It doesn't serve them or you to place yourself in another's position. Accept where others are, what they choose, how they engage, what they do, and what they create. It is their path, and this applies to their physical and emotional suffering."*

Reflections

Suffering for one may not be for another. Do not try to place yourself in another's position. It is wasteful of your energy and does not serve the other person. Love and compassion for another is wonderful; placing yourself in another's position is not. That person has his or her path and you have yours. The suffering you see may be satisfaction of a karmic debt or an opportunity to learn and grow. We do not know.

Dane Boggs

Friends Departure

Ivo said, *"A successful departure. She is golden light. She feels very queen beeish! It's a play on words. Her energy is very draped. She is covering and caring for many that she loves and supports. The draping will extend as she moves forward on her path."*

Reflections

I miss my dear friend and our talks.

Latitudinal Shift, May 3, 2016

Ivo said, *"There is a latitudinal shift occurring in the universe at this time. Those who are most sensitive to it will, of course, more greatly feel its impact. Now, in this moment, is the time to take care of you. Determine only that which is needed now, and do your best to be of service to yourself. This will pass. You will later have a different experience of life. For now, pay attention to the now, you, and your relationship to it. Breathe deeply when you know nothing else to do. It will bring some relief.*

"Usually one might say, 'Hang on. It's one hell of a ride.' These circumstances call for detachment ... holding things loosely, and trusting in your ability to get to the other side. Now is to have your focus. All else will unfold very naturally as the universe moves into a deeper but higher state of existence.

"It is mostly a process of hills and valleys, and its effect are unique and distinct to the individual. To distract yourself with its completion negates the intention to be in the now. Remember this."

Reflections

My Channel said, "Ivo sent the message to help each not feel alone in it, which creates isolation. He encourages the power of the present moment so as to ease and move through it freely, as free as we are capable of. This is easier for some than others. Acceptance versus resistance is better."

This was a very difficult time for me. Feeling out of sorts and not being able to find balance was very disturbing. Somehow I got through with Ivo's advice and counseling.

Eagle

My Channel sees an eagle following and assisting me until November of 2016. Ivo said, *"It is here at this time to assist your spiritual vision and perception providing different viewpoints and vantages. This is not unusual for animal assistance. The eyesight of the eagle is beyond measure."*

Reflections

Blessed. Thank you.

Butterfly Exchange...

You can watch the Butterfly Exchange video on my website, www.reikimaster-daneboggs.com. This happened when my wife and I were hiking along a stream in California. I felt compelled to reach down and touch a butterfly. Soon we were best of friends. He didn't want to let go. Thank you, spirit.

https://www.youtube.com/results?search_query=butterfly+exchange

Reflections

Ivo said, *"Your vibrational pull attracted the butterfly. A connective fusion occurred between the two of you where energetically you were in harmony. The butterfly felt very comfortable. You had a harder time being in the moment because you kept waiting for it to change, where the butterfly was just in the moment. It's unusual for any purely wild creature to allow for such close proximity. It was trusting of you, which is out of the ordinary."*

Clip-on Wings

Ivo said, *"You will have an eye-opening moment on your upcoming trip west, validating and reinforcing your position. You have had these types of moments before. You will have distinct and conscious awareness that is unique and special with encouragement for the continuum that is needed. You will have a lift that life is worth living. The knowing part of you will be recognized. In a sense, you will have clip-on wings letting you go for a ride and see things from a different perspective. It will be an eye-opening experience. You will be given wings for a brief time, with no limitation on what you see."*

Reflections

I was standing by a gate in Gunnison, Colorado, when my wings arrived. On a conscious level, I was able to see and feel the beauty of earth. It was a special moment, with an awareness and appreciation for All That Is.

Ivo said, *"You retained but left the physical body. You left your body for a few moments. You wanted to stretch your framework. Extend and expand the energy of you, and a higher elevation was needed. The higher elevation played a part in why it happened in Colorado. It was a boost, extending your parameters. There was an increase in vibration creating heightened awareness, which allowed you to profoundly experience. This was arranged by your soul. It was a purposeful intention. When you sleep and meditate, it happens all the time. Being awake and aware is not typical. Humans normally set time aside for this activity.*

"The soul is not more important than the physical body. They are of equal importance, but the soul has access to more knowledge and awareness and is more capable in ways than the physical body by itself. You showed up and allowed. You were accepting and participating. Conscious knowledge and purpose were not necessary."

Teaching

My Channel said, "Ivo wants to acknowledge your teaching component. When you allow it, it comes very naturally. If you use your head too much, it can make it more challenging. Teaching is very natural for you. He thanks you for your willingness to teach. It is a hallmark of great measure. It's a signpost along the way. It's also encouraging for you." Ivo said, *"Be who you are and allow who you are to be seen and heard. It opens many doors for many people. People will not hear the same thing in the same way."*

Reflections

Teaching brings me great pleasure. I appreciate the assistance from the other side. Sharing is very important for my overall health and wellbeing. It allows my inner truth to be expressed and manifested in the physical world.

Fear Wallop

On our drive to North Carolina, I felt compelled to stop at a rest area. I wanted to go home. I felt so crappy, anxious, and afraid. Was I suffering from another latitudinal shift or Huntington's disease? Ivo said, *"You were scarred. This was something that had built up slowly, though it may have appeared sudden to you. You felt like the rug had been pulled out from under you. Fear can be like a wallop. You couldn't go forward without paying attention to yourself. You treated yourself in a tender and caring way with the Rife machine. The following day you received three phone calls. They gave you the opportunity to choose on where you wanted to be. They were divinely operated calls. You had a choice. You could stay in fear or answer the requests. You used those calls as a tool for promotion. It is hard to combat fear when you feel powerless. Consider using some new tools for balance. New places require new tools, assets, and recipes for greater stability and comfort."*

Reflections

It was a rough time for me. Not knowing whether I was suffering from Huntington's disease got the best of me. Ivo said, *"Don't let fear direct your life."* How lucky am I to have Ivo, my guides, and a Rife machine?

Muscle Testing 2

Muscle testing is the ability to get information from All That Is. Ivo said, *"More than anything it has to do with pure intention. It will not always be what you anticipate or expect. Pure intention is the key to effectiveness. It shows what is for the highest good of that person, pet, or situation. A request can be off course. Muscle testing requires that you are conscious of your attunement. Be conscious of yourself as part of All That Is. Be willing to be utilized as a tool where your conscious intention is pure.*

"Muscle testing is not completely different from Reiki. From an individual perspective, it may appear as giving Reiki but really an attunement to all. Any sort of a conscious attunement to all is likely to take a toll on the physical body. There is going to be an effect on the body anytime you consciously are aware of that attunement in an intentional way. It's different for each person and each circumstance. Sometimes it is fatiguing and sometimes energizing. The physical body has a certain vibration, and conscious attunements shift the vibration."

Reflections

Muscle testing allows me to gain information from All That Is for the benefit of others. For example, I can select specific auto channels and frequencies on the Rife machine for my clients as well as myself and pets. This can be a wonderful resource for those suffering from different health issues. Why shoot in the dark with the Rife machine when we can use specific auto channels and frequencies for faster healing? Answers are received from All That Is regarding what is best for each individual and each situation—not just what to run, but how often, how long, and the proper power setting. The time to get well is reduced. Remember, healing only occurs when and where it is appropriate. Each soul has its own path to follow.

HD—Huntington's Disease

I was diagnosed with HD in 2004. My mother and brother died from this horrible disease. My repeat number is forty. On January 22, 2016, I was blessed with the following *Neuroscience* article. "Neuroprotective Effects

Of Extremely Low-Frequency Electromagnetic Fields On A Huntington's Disease Rat Model: Effects On Neurotrophic Factors And Neuronal Density." See the appendix.

The abstract shows considerable potential for extremely low-frequency electromagnetic fields as a therapeutic tool for Huntington's disease. After reading this encouraging article, I muscle tested myself for HD and came up with the following frequencies for treatment and prevention: 690, 484, 986, 430, 658, 744, 577, 275, 803, 660, 682, 322, 784, 880, 428, 764, 637, 657, 1565, 2, 728, 433, 528, 60. Huntington's chorea frequencies are: 2250, 3910, 9750, 30800, 26125, 30167, 33333, 39877, 38183, 33860.

I started feeling anxious and agitated for extended periods of time in 2016. I was on an emotional roller coaster. I knew the HD monster was reaching out to get me as it had done with my mother and brother. I started using the frequencies above on April 15, 2016 and felt better right away. They seem to decrease the build up of excess HD protein. I have used them and the Rife machine every day since and will continue most likely for the rest of my life. Most HD people will need the Rife machine the remainder of their lives to treat the disease.

I suggest that anyone diagnosed or suffering with HD utilize these frequencies to minimize and reduce the disease and it's symptoms. The use of the how often the frequencies are run, how long, and the proper power settings should be determined prior to using a Rife machine. Repeats of the frequencies above and gating on the machine also need to be considered. Sometimes the frequencies above don't need to be run at all. Try to find a gifted and qualified person to answer these questions.

Reflections

Ivo said, *"The HD treatment is an offering and contribution for others in effecting and influencing the vibrational positioning of the whole being. Availing oneself to an optional vibration gives each individual an opportunity to adjust and alter one's vibration. Sometimes it works, and sometimes it may not. The offering is there to support the vibrational change or not. Some will choose to create a change, and some will not."*

Healing only occurs when it is appropriate for each individual. Sometimes the soul does not want to heal.

"The universe is not conceptual. All is energy. All is vibration. All is varying levels of vibration. Everything is influenced by energy. Releasing expectations is tough for humans. Each individual is unique."

New Position

My Channel saw a new light springing forth from me. Ivo said, *"Your intention was to demonstrate light in a different way. Thank you for that transformation, upgrading and enhancing your contribution and influences. You have had some bumpy times recently. Now that you have arrived and achieved this position, the challenge will be less. It was more physical than emotional for you. It was a struggle."*

Reflections

The last year has been difficult for me. The recent passing of my brother brought the reality of HD front and center. Losing my ability to stay centered and balanced was frightening. A fear wallop combined with latitudinal shifts put me in a dark place. Finding the *Neuroscience* article brought me hope that specific frequencies could cure my HD. The daily treatments relaxed me immediately, but it's taken about a year to feel better. It had to be done slowly and carefully. I now realize I was much sicker than I thought. HD was sneaking up on me in small, incremental ways without my knowledge. I can look back and see happenings that were HD related. I am so blessed to have a Rife machine, a tool to keep HD and other illnesses away. The Rife machine cured me of Lyme disease and is helping me fight Huntington's. It is my prayer that others embrace this technology for themselves and their families.

Ascension

Ivo said, *"Ascension is what normally happens after one leaves the physical body. Some souls are now creating ascension while in the physical body. You are one of them. Souls are now inhabiting the planet who have the ability to ascend and maintain presence in the physical body. Evolved souls are choosing to return to earth with this intention of creating ascension and maintaining the physical body simultaneously. This alters and changes the vibration of the soul beyond what is typical in the physical world. Human bodies are not made for ascension, to transcend without leaving the body behind, where the body accompanies the soul and energy on its journey. Ascension here on earth can assist us all and is a good thing. People are staying where before they left, sharing that it can be done, guiding others in the same possibilities. It's occurring and is in existence. The more success there is, the more there can be. Ascension can happen again and again.*

Bodies are capable of experiencing vibrations that are higher now, moving beyond what is typical of the past. Ascension is an elevation in vibration. Bodies are functioning and maintaining existence at higher vibration, extending and ascending. Ascension used to occur when bodies were no longer living, now some physical bodies are stretching themselves to hold that higher vibration. Remember the whole of you is not your body. The higher self is an aspect of you that is not held in the body. Ascension is extending and expanding the vibration of your essence while maintaining a connection to the physical body. This in turn raises the vibration of the planet. This is progress for the human species.

We do not know how each physical body is going to respond to the process. You are well familiar with physical anomalies. You are in that process. Steady yourself with something strong, stable and secure when you feel its effects. Give attention and focus to that identified object and connection. The longer you stay in the physical the more the physical body requires that it become familiar with the unfamiliar. Your new normal keeps changing. There is a level of service that you are contributing and providing by being willing to be part of this experiment. You wanted to know this consciously, not for preparation. You have everything you need—no added extra effort or attention needed. It is a profound and new ground for you."

Reflections

I wish to be of service.

God Is Not a Concept!

Ivo said, *"All is of God. All at its core is pure. The essence of all is pure, and transformations occur in all capacities and directions. It is karmic based. It depends on a soul's history. The best approach is not assessing things as good or bad but recognizing that to all comes benefit. That can be hard as a human being when something is painful, tragic, horrific, or cruel. Life experiences create an opportunity to grow, evolve, and transform to a higher capacity and position. When we feel pain, it may create a transformation within us that alters our purity. When we feel afraid, it may create a transformation within us that alters our purity. It appears we are less pure. Our actions, what we say, and what we do can come from a less-pure place. When we feel love, we know how to experience it, and it enhances our purity. Every experience gives one an opportunity of choice. Exercise choice with divine purity and love. It is beyond the conceptual mind to comprehend. It is more recognizing that all is of God. Everything brings about benefit to the benefit of all. There are things to learn, to change, to grow. Even when something horrible happens, wonderful things can come from it. It is beyond the conceptual mind to acknowledge. The mind has limitations that anticipate or expect it to make sense and be understood. We cannot put God into conceptual terms. As humans, that's what you like to do. God is not a concept."*

Reflections

God is not a concept.

IVO SPEAKS

Ivo's first words to my channel were, *"I am God light."* Ivo speaks to my channel from the nonphysical world. These are his words that I have transcribed from our three-way conversations. Let his words of wisdom, compassion, and love bring you greater comfort and peace. We do not need to suffer as we do.

This section requires time to read and understand. Let Ivo's words become part of your conscious self. Let them filter into your day-to-day activities. Your divine self already has this knowledge. Bring this knowledge—*the truth*—into your current life. You will be glad you did. Become more enlightened.

Abortion

If a pregnancy ends through miscarriage or abortion, the soul looks elsewhere or waits in that circumstance.

Absence

It is not necessary to justify absence, but it is okay if you do.
It is helpful to know that it is not necessary.
Embrace your choices, whatever they are.
Sometimes justification is a waste of energy and time for everyone.

Ascension

Ascension is what normally happens after one leaves the physical body.
Some souls are now creating ascension while in the physical body.

Souls are now inhabiting the planet who have the ability to ascend and maintain presence in the physical body.

This alters and changes the vibration of the soul beyond what is typical in the physical world.

Human bodies are not made for ascension, to transcend without leaving the body behind, where the body accompanies the soul and energy on its journey.

Evolved souls are choosing to return to earth with this intention of creating ascension and maintaining the physical body simultaneously.

Ascension here on earth can assist us all and is a good thing.

People are staying where before they left, sharing that it can be done, guiding others in the same possibilities.

t's occurring and is in existence.

The more success there is, the more there can be.

Ascension can happen again and again.

Aliens

Our alien visitors are mostly curious and helpful.
There is nothing inherently evil about them.
There is a broad existence.
There are many different levels of energy.
There are many different dimensions.
The earth is not the center of it all.

All

Reiki masters attune us to all.
*The attunement to **all** is the intention and purpose, acknowledging oneself as **all**.*
*Reiki masters remind us of **all** we are and **all** we know.*

All

Hold and grasp hands with all.
Feel your connection to all.
Nothing serves your soul like a reminder of this interconnection.
Nothing serves you greater.

Serve yourself well.
Get everything that you need and all that is in full support of you.
Sometimes this involves asking others for assistance.
That's the resonation.

All

Continue an interest in knowing yourself within you rather than aside of you.
Within you is by way of you.
Aside of you is looking elsewhere.
*Connect to **God** by way of self.*
Discover all.
*Your connection to **all** is by way of you.*
*Everything and **all** is within you.*
Don't leave yourself behind.
It is a common distraction.
All** is not **all** without **you.
All requires you.
All is inclusive of self.

All

***All** is as it needs to be.*
There is no way it couldn't be.
Sometimes it is near to impossible in our human existence to see this truth.
Such a sense of complexity to existence.
It is beyond comprehension.
Create a position that is more accepting and peaceful.
All is just.
All is of balance. All is divine.
All is God.

All Life Is Sacred

Honor and respect are of the highest importance and significance.
It's all about balance, harmony, and symmetry.
Create balance or disconnect from the practice.
Consciousness is a significant aspect of it.

Some people are uncomfortable with consciousness.
Do what creates balance.
Create an intention that is supported by balance.
Intention is sacred.
It's not about life and life forms as much as intention, honor, respect, balance, and symmetry.
In true form, there are those that come to life with the purpose of sustaining life for others, ingesting, guiding, directing, or supporting.
It is specific to each as their own.
The symmetry of existence cannot be determined by an assemblage of what is right for all.

All That Is

*We are **all that is**.*

All That Is

*Rooting within connects one to **all that is**.*
*Courage allows one to behold oneself as **all that is**.*
*Trust oneself as part of **all that is**.*
Look beyond independence and individuality.
*Look beyond that because we are **all that is**.*
Give yourself the proper opportunity to reveal yourself.

Art

Art sends out divine energy.

Assimilation

Between lives, one recognizes what one gave and what one received.
It is a play-by-play catch-up.
One waits for the proper opportunity to return.
Time is well spent.
One prepares and assimilates for reentry.

Attachment

Do not experience any attachment to birth or death, destruction or invention.
Attachment can create a feeling of torture, misery, angst, and hardship.
Get rid of personal attachments.
Experience the flow.
There is power in this choice.

Audience

The audience is as important as you, whether one or thirty people.
It is important to have some sense of structure when you put yourself in front
*   of an audience.*
Honor the experience by preparing, but be in the moment and be guided by
*   everyone present.*
It may be spoken or unspoken.
Speak from the heart.
By honoring yourself, you honor all.

Bad Things

Bad things happen.
We cannot expect the human mind and heart to find acceptance.
Remember, there is always a bigger picture.
What appears to be is not only what is.
Remember, karma is always balancing.
There is always justice and balance.
September 11, 2001, was a monumental, horrific event.
Many chose to give up their lives.
It changed so many people and things.
More good came out of it than bad.
An outpouring of love raised the consciousness and vibration of the planet.

Balance

The more balance one retains, the greater one's ability and offering.

Balance

When you are in a place of greater balance, everything benefits.

Balance

One can bring balance to whatever imbalance is occurring.
A huge part of this is one's ability to be more fluid.

Balance

Balance does not look one way.
Be aware of yourself in a constant and near way.
No one else can determine your balance.
Circumstances and positions of balance that worked in the past may work no
*   longer.*
Navigate the world with balance in mind.
Balance supports, promotes, and creates circumstances and opportunities.
Support your balance in a consistent manner.

Barriers and Hurdles

Barriers cannot be crossed.
A hurdle, by way of its nature, is to be crossed.
Some things are placed in your life's path so you can overcome them.
Some things are placed in your life's path to divert you.
It has to do with your attention and perception to identify both or either
*   correctly.*
If fear is present, it's a red flag for a hurdle.
Put the fear to the side.
It's nearly impossible to jump a hurdle if fear is present.
Set the fear aside so you can look at things more clearly.
A barrier quality is insistence.
Insistence in its own way is resistance.
Don't be blinded by insistence.
A barrier rarely has fear, and a hurdle rarely has insistence.
Insistence is isolating.
*Moving forward in a lone way is different from moving forward with **all***
*   **that is.***

Beauty and Perfection

*See the beauty and perfection of **all**.*
*Be open to the perfection of **all**.*
See the perfection that is unique and distinct to each.
Everything is perfect, even if it is uncomfortable and painful.
Don't get caught up in your chosen perceptions.
Step outside the human regard of perfection.
Do not judge.

Behind Bars

Anytime you find yourself restricted or limited, simply change your position.
Stand in a different place, move yourself, and get a different perspective.
Be where you are differently.
You have the ability to choose different dynamics, elements, and perspectives.
Darkest moments are when you need to remember this choice.
There is always something else available.
There are always options.

Be in the Moment

Not being in the moment is like leaving yourself alone,
abandoned, stripped bare, deleted, and depleted.
Awareness and willingness in the moment will support and serve you.
When you give yourself permission to be who you are, where you are, so do you
*   find yourself bringing all that you are capable of to that moment.*
This is functioning at your highest capacity.

Bird of Flight

If one feels hesitant or restricted, attune oneself to a bird of flight.
When you find peace with your moments, it allows you to move freely to the
*   next.*

Birth and Death

Sometimes when conception occurs, souls start lining up.
There are different criteria and lessons to be learned.

Once the soul is assigned by the divine, contact is made with the parents.
The soul does not enter the body until birth.
The soul of the baby attaches when the body of the mother no longer supports the baby.
It takes a soul to sustain life.
The soul of the body comes and goes when the baby is young but is always attached.
A process of assimilation occurs between the body and soul.
When one nears death through old age and illness, the soul moves in and out of the body to visit the other side.
One end is much like the other.

Body

Bring attention to your body and posture.
Adjust your body as needed.
It will support your overall balance.
More ease is created by practicing awareness.
Practice greater body consciousness.
Retrain your body.
When you are tired or fatigued, have the grace to rest.

Body

The body has amazing healing potential that cannot be explained.

Boundaries

You can live your life within the realms of intellectual understanding, like a scientist or you can live a life filled with magic and miracles.
Celebrate the miracles.
They will stoke your curiosity and interest, inviting you to broaden your boundaries.
If you feel safety and security only come from understanding, then you limit your life experiences to a capacity of intellectual contribution.

Bounty

Allow yourself the grace, beauty, and existence of each day.
You deserve to feel treasured by you.
The bounty of good will that comes from you toward others and self is divinely based.
Validate and support the divine presence within you.
Take good care of yourself and the opportunities this life brings.

Capacity

It is common for one to gravitate toward one who shares a similar capacity.
There is support, inspiration, and offerings in this interaction.
It has nothing to do with one's position and status in the world but one's essence.

Challenges

All lives have challenges and accomplishments.
Challenges and difficulties are a matter of individual perception.
Acknowledge the evolution of your existence.

Chatter

There is so much chatter in the world.
It's your choice what you bring in.
Create balance for yourself.
All chatter is absorbed on some level.
Everyone is exposed.
Some feel invigorated while some feel exhausted.
A different level of consciousness is exhibited by each.
Some let go, some download, and some digest.
There is a vastness in exploration and exposure.

Choice

See the beauty and profoundness of existence.
Focus on all that is grand.
It encourages one to a better place.
It's all about choice.

Cloning

Cloning is a physical reproduction.
It is man created instead of God created.
Manmade replication has lots of faults and missing components.
There can never be an exact replication.

Comfort

Comfort need not come from familiarity.
Comfort can come from attunement and alignment that is distinct to you.
Do not hold yourself to past parameters.
It's all about comfort.
There is a difference between ease and easy.
It's an experience of perfection.

Confrontation

Don't go in with an attitude.
Say what you need or what works for you.
Be willing to face things straight on.
Say, "This doesn't work for me!"
There is a difference between confrontation and conflict.
Confront in a pure way.
This will provide the greatest opportunity for accomplishing your objectives.

Connections

Soul attachments can occur.
This is called a connection.
Two souls cannot be in the same body, but one can accompany another.
An attachment is where a soul tries to attach to a body that it was not assigned.
This cannot occur if the soul and body maintain a sense of power.
One's belief and acceptance can create and encourage the probability.
Fear weakens.
Sometimes what is occurring is misunderstood or perceived incorrectly.
Nothing dark is occurring.
It's just a wayward soul that is lost, confused, or unsure.

Just say, "This is mine. Go away."
Nothing and no one has more power over you than yourself.

Consciousness

Being in the moment encourages consciousness.
You are abandoning yourself if you step outside the moment.
You are stripping yourself bare.
The opportunity for consciousness in the moment is greatly reduced if you are not there.
Depletion can occur.

Contracts

Contracts are sometimes defined and sometimes very broad.
If people are trusting, then contracts are less structured.
If people are less trusting, then contracts are more structured.
It has to do with one's track record.

Conveyance

Conveyance can be done soul to soul.
You do not have to do it in a physical way.
It is safer for some and more comfortable if soul to soul.

Curiosity

Curiosity is an active opening.
Curiosity invites things to you beyond the realm of expectation and awareness.
There is an energy to it that compels and encourages movement.

Death

Rarely are there accidental deaths.
Long illnesses give the soul an opportunity to wrap up loose ends.
Souls make their own departure decisions.
Someone else cannot make it.

Death

When people die, they do not stay that age or in that place.
Don't hold on to the relationship that existed at death.
That was one moment in time.
Don't get stuck on something that no longer exists.
Detach and let your loved one's heavenly presence be more profoundly and beautifully experienced.
The relationship is not severed when the body dies.
The relationship continues.
Open hearts create broader awareness.
The more healing your heart is capable of, the more freedom the departed one gets.

Death

When someone dies, it is not wrong.
Accidents are not wrong.
What occurs is not wrong.
You can't say it's right, but you can say it's not wrong.
For example, 9/11 was a light to the world.

Deletion

Don't loiter in the future.
This can create a large energetic deficit.
Do not overextend and delete yourself.

Detaching

Be conscious of attachments.
Things don't need to be any one way.
Projections can lead to disappointments.
Be conscious of detaching.

Detachment

Detachment supports the progression of one's journey.

Detachment

Humans are guided by pain and pleasure.
Detachment supports fluidity and movement.
Attachment inhibits fluidity and movement.
Whatever one experiences in any given moment is for one's highest good.
This recognition will reduce one's tendency to be attached.
Recognize all things and circumstances as opportunities.
They support the breadth and depth of one's experiences.
Everything in life that occurs brings about benefit.
It's easy to see when it is comfortable.

Departure

Departure is between one's soul and God.
Everyone is on their way to departure.
Some departures are near and some are far.
There are as many varieties on departure orientation and method as there are human beings.
Each departure is fit for one's needs and goals.

Departure

Every departure is unique to itself.
Sometimes they are predetermined prior to birth.
Sometimes it is determined while in the body.
Sometimes it is a matter of circumstance or situation.
It is a matter of life and happens in the course of living.
It would not occur if it was wrong.

Departures

Departures are not accidents.
When a person goes, it's okay for him or her to go.
Often when one is struck with grief, comprehension is not wanted.
Sometimes we do not want to accept it.

Devil

The devil is a human representation of evil or bad.

Devotion and Dedication

Let devotion and dedication to self grow.
We are basically all doing the same thing.
It is helpful to identify that all are participating in the same process, but all experience it from their own unique positions.
When you grasp this, you have ultimate compassion for others and yourself.
As humans, we have a tendency to assume others' actions and personal capacity from our position.

Disasters

Nothing is outside of God.
Disasters are attention gathering.
More global unity occurs.
This cajoling raises the vibration of the planet.
Even though there is great heartache in these experiences, there is more gained than lost.
Disasters cannot really be explained, but they create the broadest opportunity for all.
One needs to embrace that those souls may no longer be needed and may not need to return.

Distinct and One

We have a physical body, we are individuals, and we have specific bodies and humanness, but that is not who we are.
We are distinct and one at the same time.

Distractions

The processes and intentions of others can be a distracting dynamic.
You cannot disconnect from God, but you can get distracted.
Do not let go of the covenant relationship with self.

Do not involve yourself outwardly in a non balanced way.
It's all about gathering an ability to temper and balance.

Divine

All is divine.

Divine

Life is divine.
Acknowledge the divine in the simplest of forms and circumstances.
This will open many doors.
See all as divine.
Be willing to witness the divine.
Accept the offerings.
There are opportunities that surround us constantly.
This is the music of life.

Dogs

Souls of dogs have equal status to humans.
The progression of dogs is very similar to the souls that inhabit human bodies.
Humans often find their greatest inspiration by way of such creatures.
One can be oneself in the company of such purity.
Nature, animals, and babies inspire us as well.

Donation

Organ donation is a fairly recent circumstance that creates an opportunity for
*   greater expansion.*
Sometimes organs are donated to others who are familiar with the donor on
*   a soul level.*
Some souls donate and walk away.
Some souls donate and stick around.
Some souls validate a previous connection, and some create a new one.
Increased longevity has opened the door to re-upping and walk-ins.

Doubt

Doubt in its simplest capacity is an opportunity for a second look.
Be open to opportunities that doubt provides.
It can support you and give you more clarity.
Do not banish it.
Perceive doubt as a friend.

Drag

We are all growing and evolving all the time, whether consciously involved
    or not.
With intention it is greater.
Human beings experience soul growth.
You cannot revert or go backward.
When one puts pressure or puts effort into growth, it can create a drag.
Sometimes effort creates heaviness.

Earth

It is all vibrational based.
There are varying rounds of vibration.
Different forms and energies can affect and influence.
There continue to be outer influences that are not of this world.
Outer influences do not have the same vibration as the earth plane.
Human projections are very limited as to what it's all about, because the human
    mind does not have the capacity or ability to comprehend it.
Possibilities are endless.

Earth

Never has there been a time when the earth has held such a population.
Human presence does create an effect.
Earth is a place where great soul advancement can occur.
There is a growing sense of human-to-human connectedness.
We are in this together.
Progress may not appear to you, but it is in evidence.

Ego

Ego is a reflection of our humanness.
Step away from it.
Less ego allows the heart to expand.

Ego

You cannot separate your ego from human nature.
You cannot separate your essence from your presence.
There is something beneficial about every aspect of you.
Accept and embrace all aspects.
It's all about balance.

Enlightenment

The pineal gland is affected by enlightenment.
Enlightenment is an indication of progression.
Enlightenment is not a destination; it's a process.
One can experience enlightenment from different positions.
It's what occurs as you grow and expand.
It's personal movement that is supported and encouraged from within.
More than one dynamic is available.
The process is unique and distinct for each person.
There are all kinds of different forms of unfolding.
Enlightenment doesn't look one way.

Essence

Understand with your essence instead of your mind.

Essence

Everything that one thinks, feels, and experiences creates a marker on one and
*   one's essence.*

Essence

Essence is the true substance of you.

It's your soul.
It's your spirit.
It's your presence.
It's divine, eternal, true, and pure.
Sometimes people are not attuned to their essence.
Sometimes the essence is not apparent or evident because things are cloaking it
   or on top of it, but it is always true to form.
Other things can be practiced or developed.
Often those things can disregard the essence.
Life's circumstances or interactions with others can throw one off center.
Consider this as disorientation, lacking stability and security.
When one connects with oneself at the level of essence, it has a soothing,
   comforting, and calming effect.
Reiki gives each an opportunity to experience and access that essence.
It acts as a reminder of who we are.
Reiki energy is divine in nature.
Meditations can create the same kind of offerings.
It's all about being able to experience and recall the truth of you.

Fashion

Do not fashion yourself after another.
There is no one to copy.

Fatigue

Everything is energy.
Physical stamina and energy are different.
Not all energy you possess needs to be used physically.
Physical fatigue is responsive to the level of care and balance you experience.
Bodies need rest.
It has to do with balance.
We create all kinds of manners and ways to stay balanced.
It is not so much about following patterns and routines.
It can be done consciously and subconsciously.
It's all about serving yourself well.

Fatigue

Fatigue is anything that doesn't nourish the soul.
Do not let yourself be called outside of yourself.
It is important to serve from within.
Let others find their own strength.
Do not dissipate energy to the past or future.
Do not step out of the now.

Favor

Recognize your achievements.
Favor yourself.

Favor Yourself

No audience necessary.
Be attentive and favoring.
Be with yourself in a conscious regard.
What tends to be subconscious is judgment and ridicule.
There's more heckling on the subconscious level than there is favoring.
Tooting your own horn can encourage this activity on a subconscious level.
Favor yourself.

Fear

Do not let fear control your life.
Feeding fear is bad.
Being more plain and pure promotes neutrality.
Be aware of your feelings and worries, but do not allow them to direct your life.

Flexibility

Sometimes it behooves one to be flexible.
What is proper at one time may change.
Give yourself the opportunity to fluctuate.
Move about the world in a way that caters and supports you.
It can be very unproductive to cling to a prior dynamic.
Hold it loosely.

Do not become attached to a particular system or pattern.
You are organic and alive.
You are changing and flowing at every moment.
No repetition or familiar thing is needed.
What is new and different may likely be a better fit.

Flow

Go with the flow.
Don't let the mind interfere.
Be a willing participant.
Don't try to manage and control.
Trust in your ability.
You have everything you need.

Flow

A flow that is created can encourage and carry one further.
One needs awareness and willingness.
Allow and be a part of that which is flowing.

Free and Clear

Divine purity is the result of being free and clear.

Funny

Create the opportunity to laugh.
Constant reverence is not necessary.
See the humor.
Laughter is a pure expression of self and joyful freedom without inhibitions.
Laughter can create cleansing, purification, and divine expressions.
Laughter is a release broadening your own perspective.

Gather

Everything you gather supports you.
Some are temporary, and others are for life.

Awareness, understanding, awards, etc., may be short-lived.
What is needed will stay around.

Gathering

What one needs, one consciously gathers.
What one needs will not be the same as another.

Generosity

Sometimes we have a tendency to be overgenerous.
Bring attention to not neglecting yourself in such offerings.
Don't compromise yourself.
The purity of the generosity is compromised if it does not serve you as well, if it excludes you.

Gift

Not needing to grasp and understand the unexplainable can be a great gift.
Be in the world in a way that promotes and delivers dynamics that extend beyond your understanding.
Experience miracles.
Utilization of this gift depends on where a person is and the importance of control.

God

God is not a concept.
God is within you.
All that is, is within you.
It's all self-possessed.

God's Work

God's work is the way to be healthy and happy.
Be your pure self.
Be a reflection of divinity.

Grace

Create ease with your soul.
This allows you to experience more with less trauma.
Acceptance, grace, and peace are better ways of furthering.
Grace doesn't eliminate pain, but it does provide a broader perspective.

Greatest Offering

There is beauty in unwasted moments and in being able to utilize one's energy
for the greatest offering.

Grounding

It needs to suit you and where you are.
Do whatever works for you—for example, inhaling earth energy up and
exhaling earth energy back.
Walk consciously on the earth.
Sense and feel the contact.
Yoga can be very grounding.
Hold earth energy more consistently.
The activity of yoga and qigong are very grounding and stabilizing.
The grounding helps you be more stable in your own way, with regard to places,
people, and things that are not yours.

Growth

An open heart and ears make growth possible.

Growth

Internal growth processes and movement can be externally prompted.
Conscious decisions can support unconscious movement and progression.
One can disassociate oneself from where one has been.
This invites one's future and heading more quickly.

Happiness

You are worthy of happiness.

We are deserving of happiness.
We do not have to earn it.
It is our essence.

Heaven and Hell

Heaven is soulful continence.
Hell is soulful disappointment.

Heckling

Don't heckle yourself.
Be careful what you say to yourself.
Thoughts are energy.
When you think to yourself, it's loud and clear.
Be conscious and cautious of any heckling.
It's abusive.

Hell

Hell is a place of disappointment and discouragement, not a physical place.
Hell is a dissatisfied soul.
It is a soul that did not utilize the opportunity to support the divine and the whole.

Help

You can always ask for help.
Help is provided when it is needed.

Higher Self

Your higher self is the whole of you.
It cannot be held by the body.
It's not an issue of volume.
Don't think spatial!
Souls are not spatial.
Don't try to put something that is not physical into the physical realm.

Incidents

Incidents prompt learning, development, and opportunity.
We create for ourselves that which best supports our divine unfolding.
For some it is pain.
For others it is camaraderie, support, and encouragement.
It comes to us in varying forms.
The objective is the same: to support one's furthering.

Influences

There continues to be outer influences that are not of this world.
Outer influences do not have the same vibration as the earth plane.

Insistence and Resistance

Insistence is resistance.
Create an existence without resistance.
Be in the flow, with endless possibilities.
Release expectations.

Intellect

Intellect uses logic, rationality, and reason.
Intuition is acceptance.
Intellect uses more energy.
One's energy can increase if one uses less intellect.

Intention and Effort

There is a difference between intention and effort.
Effort can create an energy that repels and interferes.
In the Moment
Take your time being in the moment as thoroughly, fully, and completely as
*   you are capable.*
It gives homage to all.
Give every place that you are your attentiveness, acknowledging its value and
*   significance.*
Give whatever you are doing your full focus.

Give it its proper due.
Experience where you are and everything it offers.
It alleviates the human tendency to assess and judge by way of value or
importance.

Journey

Do not discount any of your journey.
The path is different for all of us.
Do not judge.
It is a process.

Judgment

Do not fall into a state of judgment.
Do not berate or judge your previous choices; simply learn from them.
All steps are important.
Ask yourself, "How might I choose to do it differently next time?"
Educate and prepare yourself for future gatherings.
Remain positive for you and your processes.
Do not turn on yourself in any way, shape, or form.
To regret, judge, or ridicule a past position only creates distrust within yourself.
Remain supportive, encouraging, and comforting all the days of your life.
It's important to remain positive and supportive of self.
Acknowledge the progress you are making.
Support yourself in the most thorough way.

Justification

Justification is personal.
When considering justification, you must go with your own.
We each have our own truth.
You cannot allow another truth to create wavering from your own.
It diminishes the world of a pure you.
It challenges you in a way that brings inhibition.
Judgments, expectations, and obligations can be very distracting.

Karma

There is more than meets the eye.
No one knows what the introduction or completion of karma is.

Knowledge

You are universal knowledge.
You know everything already.

Leaders

A good leader supports and encourages.
*A great leader finds a way to help others connect to their source, helping others
    to find, to know, and to access their own source.*
A great leader helps others feel and find more comfort in this world.

Learning

Learning can take place on a physical and soul level.
It can occur when the soul is out of the body.
Learning can occur when we revisit positions of the past from a new perspective.

Leavings

Leavings are remnants, leftovers, things you disregard.
Be willing to relinquish things that no longer serve a purpose.
*Willfully let go of all things that are burdensome, like ideas, thoughts, situations,
    or memories.*
Judgments and assessments may also need to be released.
Recognize this transaction.
It propels you forward.

Levels of Usefulness

As humans we judge things as more or less.
A human's perception can interfere with an offering.
It's all divinely regulated.

*One can have a profound experience with less than another would have with
    more.*
Different individuals have different opportunities and capacities.
Less can be more for some, and more can be less for others.
There are different levels of usefulness.
When things are no longer useful, they become extinct.
They conclude and become complete.

Life

Life is a powerful and complex existence.

Life

Observe the process and cycle of life that is profound.
No one place or moment is better than another.
Being in your twenties is not better than being in your nineties.
There is beauty and perfection in every part.
Reverence and respect all parts of life.

Living and Survival

There is a vast difference between living and survival.
Survival is less vibrant.
When one begins to realize the difference, survival is no longer acceptable.
Give yourself permission to experience living.
This has nothing to do with what life looks like.

Love

If there is no love, there is no love lost.
*You can choose to live without love, and you have nothing to lose, but you
    wouldn't experience your full potential.*

Love

*Love is the basic foundation of **all**.*
The seed that is planted needs water and sunshine.

The resource is there, but how active and vibrant is it?
The environment you create within you supports your ability to make use of the resource.
Think consciously so as to purposefully contribute what feeds and serves love.
All thoughts create the reality of your existence.
Be deliberate and intentional about your thoughts and beliefs so as to act with deliberateness in creating your own life.
So much of it has to do with whether you feel deserving of it.
You are.

Love

Babies are love.
Babies soak of love.

Love

It is so vitally important and essential to support a dynamic of love within and around.
The capacity of love you have for yourself, and within you, is the reservoir you have for all else.
You cannot love someone else more than you love yourself.
The love you have for yourself is the reservoir to draw upon and to share with all.
There is no substitute for love.
One must give access to gain access.
Be open enough to gain access to the depth of love that you are composed of and have the capacity for.
There are lots of distractions in life that get in the way of self-love, self-acceptance, and divine realization.
Vulnerability is the access.
It is well worth it to see and feel oneself at one's capacity.
Minimum effort gives maximum payoff.

Maladies

Physical maladies provide an opportunity to pay attention.
Most have a tendency to gather attention with pain.

The more aware and attentive you are, the better.
Trust the intuitive part of you.

Marriage

Deliver your pure self in marriage.
That honors the relationship.
Be your current self.
t's about being there.
It's not about words.
Words can sometimes interfere with the connection.
It's about exhibiting your greatest capacity in each moment.

Marriage

Let marriage be a union that is valid, strong, true, and supportive of each.
Let it be a joyful acceptance of each other's differences.
Graduate from tolerance to acceptance to celebration of one's differences.

Meditating

When meditating, let distractions fall aside.
Find a hush position.
Be available and accessible.
*Connect to **all that is**.*
It is a pure moment.
It is not better than other states.

Meditation and Sleep

The soul needs assurances.
The soul explores when it steps beyond the body.
*Only a small part of **all that is** can be known by the body.*
Sleep and meditation restore the body and soul.
The soul is never without the body, but it steps outside the body during sleep
*   and meditation.*
This restores the body and soul.
It is a pause from human existence.

The body and soul both get a break.
It's a time for just being.
The purity of one's existence is recognized.
It's helpful for humans to spend time in this state.
Know yourself as pure.
Your state of being is pure.

Miracle on the Hudson

The miracle on the Hudson supported humankind's renewal.

Mocking

Making fun of someone is disrespectful and disregarding.
If exposed, do no correction or berating; instead do the opposite.
Be thoughtful, not thoughtless.
Step in and do something different.
A shift can occur.
It must come from the heart.
It has to be true for you.
Rescuing doesn't teach anything.

Moments

Recognize and embrace that in every moment everything is unfolding anew.

Monogamous

Monogamous means personal distinction and uniqueness.
No two people are alike.
The singularity of your presence is acknowledged.
There is the distinction of one.
Think about the beauty of that.
*One can be part of **all** and distinct at the same time.*
Everything you are is exactly what you need.
People, circumstances, things you do, things you bring, and things you say and
*   take all have distinction.*
Identify your monogamy.

This supports you and your ability to deliver yourself more purely and distinctly to the world.
Your contribution is more effective and pure.

Nature

There is purity in nature.
It is a place where one is more likely to experience the purity of oneself.

Neutrality

Neutrality is a middle place.
Neutrality can be a very natural state of existence.
Part of a neutral standing is detachment and balance.

New Eyes

Use new eyes all the time.
At every step along the way, you are different.
Create an existence that is current and present.
Attend to yourself.
The past is a reference point.

Ninety-Eight Percent

About 98 percent of your decisions are predictable.
Those who assist you know you well.
You might call them traffic controllers.
They know the logistics of using your life and every part of the world to support your progression and position.
They know what you need and where you need to be.
Your choices are not unexpected.

Now

The most significant event of your life needs to be now.

Dane Boggs

Numbness

One can numb oneself during illnesses.
One can shut down certain parts of oneself.
One can release the numbness afterward for more vibrancy.

Oneness

Outside human experience, the soul has no physical body.
There is no separation.
Everyone is part of everyone.
Oneness reigns.

Oneness

All of life is about learning, development, growing, and unity.
It is about creating and experiencing oneness.

Oneness

*It's all about the existence of the **whole**.*
It's about balance, beauty, and harmony.
*It's about the existence of **all** in the midst of **all**.*
*It's the existence of **oneness** in the midst of anything.*
Oneness is something we know within ourselves.
We desire to feel and experience the oneness.
It is something we feel rather than understand.

Opportunities

Avail oneself of opportunities.
What is there for one to gather?
Hold a position that is sponge like.
***No** place is a disadvantage.*
When you are in a bad place, do not withdraw because you will be there longer.
There is always something to learn and utilize for one's furthering.

Opportunity

Sometimes you need an opportunity.
Sometimes you get where you are going without the opportunity.
We all have different routes.
They can take years or lifetimes.

Other Side

When you connect with one on the other side, you connect with the whole.
You connect with the soul and personality.
It is not something that can be separated.

Original Thought

There is no original thought.
Some people may perceive it as their idea.
You can't create anything new because it already exists.
Awareness can be new.
You can have an aha moment.

Out of Body

When you no longer need the safety and security of the body, you can experience
*   things outside the body.*
The holding of self, soul, spirit, and essence is released.
The soul has a more fluid opportunity for expansion.
It can see more broadly and less conclusively.
This contributes to epiphany.

Pain

Pain is associated with resistance to change.
With acceptance, the pain lessens.
Pain is part of living and the human experience.
Wanderings from God can also create pain.

Dane Boggs

Pain

It is amazing how much pain the human body can retain.
We still function and learn to live with it, not even aware of it.
The human resistance to releasing pain is great.
Pain is identifiable with certain situations, dynamics, and history.
Therefore, there is a tendency to accumulate and store pain.
Sometimes a slight release is accepted.

Parts

Recognize that each part of you is vital on its own and to the whole.
All parts of you are vital, significant, and important.
All of you can be conveyed by each part, no matter what you are doing.
Bring your essence through all parts.
This releases self-imposed restrictions.
One piece of you is not less of you than the whole.

Passage

You don't need to know you are ready to be ready.
The passage of the body and the passage of the soul are simultaneous but not always identical.
Trauma for the body does not necessarily mean trauma for the soul.
Trauma for the soul does not necessarily mean trauma for the body.
They are concurrent but not always identical.

Passing

All wish to feel balance, satisfaction, and contentment at their passing.
It's about contributing to the unity or disrupting it.
The soul's progression is about the unity of all.

Places

Every physical place has its own energy.
Each location has a different resonation.
We are drawn to certain places more than others.
It's a personal preference.

Everyone has unique and distinct experiences of different places.
It is the same with friendships.
Do not apply judgment.
Trust your own.

Position

Your position with self is primary.
Your position with all else is secondary.
This will give you greater comfort.
Don't let others merge and purge into your world.

Position

Hold a position that is grounded and dedicated to self.
Your actions need to be internally prompted.
Your true self allows you to hold your own.
Know your own, and everyone benefits.

Position

One's position is always valid and purposeful.
You do not need to understand where you are to be attentive.
Be supportive and encouraging of your needs.
Honor yourself.

Position

Unfair comparisons are best avoided between people.

Processes

Attention, fluidity, flexibility, and mobility with your processes grants permission
to others to do the same.
Grant others freedom in their processes so they can be who they are.

Projections

Human projections are very limited as to what it's all about because the human
*   mind does not have the capacity or ability to comprehend it.*
The possibilities are endless.
It is all vibrational based.
There are varying rounds of vibration.
As important and significant as this world is, it is a small part of the whole.

Qigong — Reiki

Qigong is an active position.
Qigong encourages the use of the body that is all about movement.
Generally people develop a practice or system that is most effective for them.
It is as unique as there are people.
No two people or processes are exactly the same.
It has to do with the tool and how it is used.
Reiki engages the body and energy in a way that is more about calm.
When you are giving Reiki to yourself, you are in a more receptive mode.
To be receptive, you must find a position for yourself that is more neutral.
Receptivity is a more vulnerable position.

Radiant Being

You are a radiant being of light.
Let yourself assume that slot, position, and placement.
Accept and allow yourself to be secure in that spot.
There are different levels of realization and acceptance.
It's a vibrational thing.
So what can you be?
What are you open to?
What can you allow?
What can you accept?
Any limitations are self-imposed.
The sky is the limit.

Relationships

Admiration has a distinct and powerful energy.

It does not have to be verbal to be beneficial; it is still delivered.
This keeps the relationship fresh and vital.
Admiration is valuable for the connection, partnership, and unification of the
relationship.

Relationships

Relationships require attentiveness by both parties.
It's important to reach toward each other for mutual effect and sharing.
It requires that both make connections on a human and soulful level.
Sometimes growth is so swift and vast that we are not aware of it.
Make eye contact on a daily basis to maintain your connection.
Eyes are the windows of the soul.
Allow each other to see the changes.
What you are capable of and willing to do changes as you grow and evolve.
Some relationships come to a place where they are done.
It's a completion.
Sometimes we have the ability to move into new worlds together.
Looking into another's eyes will lead you there if you are willing.
You will discover more about yourself and each other.

Religion

Religions are principles and practices that allow each person to find his or her
way to God.

Remembrances

Everything that you review you can review with your current self.
Don't let you past position influence your current place.
Opportunities to view it differently increase over time.
You are growing and evolving.
Something insignificant or profound can be viewed again from your new
position.
Your perception and ideas can change as you change.
When you tell a story, your perception of it can change.
Vulnerability is key, and it takes a strong one to be vulnerable.
It requires a recognition of this strength.

Increase your self-devotion and commitment to self.
Never doubt for a minute that every moment gives you what you need for the
    moment that follows.
You are not unprepared.
By the time you get there, you will have what you need.

Resistance

Resistance to movement is uncomfortable.
It's the attachment to any circumstance, position, or individual that creates the
    intensity of discomfort.
The less judgment there is, the less attachment there is, the more comfort there is.

Resource

Each of us is a resource of balance.
This contributes to the balance of all.

Review

A review occurs at the end of life.
It is a review of intention versus what has been achieved.
Anything that continues to be learned counts.
Attention is given to last-minute growing and adjustments, even in a coma.
As long as you are in your physical body, what you do, accomplish, and achieve
    counts.

Risk

You do not have to play it safe all the time.
Risk has offerings.

Safety and Security

Safety and security are not determined by external circumstance.
They are internal.
In circumstances that appear to be haphazard, it's hard to believe.

Safety

Be assured of your safety.
You are always safe.
Safety is what you hold within yourself by being committed to self.
You are safe because what you experience is always within your capacity.
If you die, you know you are safe.

Satisfaction

What satisfied one in the past may no longer satisfy one in the present.
It may not express one's fullest self.

Scorn

Scorn has no place in one's life or existence.
Cease to participate in it.
It is a poison and is destructive to that which is divinely created.
It is a meaningless energetic output.
It has no value or profitable purpose.

Seasons

There are seasons for all, as in nature.
It's best to follow your individual processes.
It's also the positioning and preparedness of others to receive.
Being alone can also contribute to the world.
Know and acknowledge your seasons.
Contribute and be accepting of your seasons.

Security

Safety and security are not compromised by fluidity.
Trust fluidity.
Dedication to self is where you find security.
Your relationship with self must take precedence.

Selective Hearing

Be very selective in what you choose to accept and believe.
Discern what you want to do with what you hear.
You have the opportunity and ability to use what you hear in the manner that
*   you see fit.*
You can engage and not engage as you desire.
Have conscious determination around what you choose to be part of in your
*   world, knowing and knowledge.*
Your hearing can be a personal selective process.
Sometimes what you hear you hear consciously and sometimes subconsciously.
Truth for another may not be truth for you.
Each holds a unique and distinct position, and each holds a perception from
*   that position that is unique and distinct.*
If you pay attention to your own, you will know where you are, and you will
*   know what stance to take, in any place, in any position, and at any time.*

Self

Be dedicated and devoted to oneself.
This will provide a great sense of security, safety, and stability.
Have a profound relationship with self.
It can be very effective and valuable.

Self

Create a trusting, supportive, and valid relationship with self.

Self

Bring who you are into every moment.
Do not diminish yourself.
Know the fullness of self.
Develop a relationship with your innermost self.
Safety, security, and stability are inward based.

Sensitivity

Overall sensitivity is a plus.

It can be inconvenient at times.
When you grow, part of your growth is an increase in vibration.
The increase in vibration is an aspect of your greater sensitivity.
Maintain a position here on earth that continues to work.

Sexuality

Some come into this world in a less-than-typical position.
Some come into this world and choose comfort with the same sex.
*The law is **all is love**.*
*It's all about what teaches you and helps you discover **love**.*

Shine

The purity of you is what affects your shine.
Everyone's capacity for shine is different.
There is a movement and shifting in the shine.
People's fluctuation in shine and radiance can be very different.
It's very alive.
Some souls have an attachment or adherence that can dim the shine.
Untruths, falsities, fears, attachments, appearances, misunderstandings, and
*   anything that is not part of your pure essence can alter the gleam of your*
*   shine.*

Shine

Embrace your shine.
Claim it.
Accept and embrace all you are.
Deliver all of you.
Acknowledge your shine.
Recognize what is pure and of God, like your essence and the love in you.
Give yourself your favor.
Less of self is just as inappropriate as more of self.

Significance

Recognize the significance of magnificence.

Every little thing has its place.
All is significant.
You can't help but include yourself.

Sleep

When you sleep, the body rests.
The soul doesn't develop fatigue like the body.

Soar

Allow yourself to soar and be utilized as a tool of God, going with the flow
    instead of against the stream.
Use your surroundings and accomplices to propel yourself.
Do not try to override things.
This creates an independent struggle.
Be like an eagle and soar.

Soul

The soul is the reference of **all**.
Souls have their own essence or flavor.
Each of us is unique and eternal.

Soul

The soul gets to choose the body it occupies.
Honor the bravery of the soul.
Experiences can be painful.
Fear is courage turned golden.
Look where the soul gets to go.
The end result is the same.
Replace pity and sorrow with admiration, respect, and reverence.
Put aside your judgment and assessment.
Choose so consciously.
It is good for them and you.
Grace usually comes when one recognizes and realizes one's capacity and ability
    to transform.

Peace comes from acceptance.
The soul meets it with enthusiasm and excitement.
Some people take a train and some take a missile.

Soul

The soul enters the body at the time of birth.
You do not separate yourself from your body until departure.
This is a soul and sole journey.

Soul Growth

Human growth and development are always associated with soul growth and development.
Human capacity is often more apparent, but it does not mean it is more important.
We have a tendency to gravitate toward similar positions of growth and development on a human and soul level.
Sometimes you engage others to enhance their growth, and sometimes you engage others to enhance your growth.
One can give and receive in different places.
The greatest growth occurs when it is mutually advantageous.
*When you are your pure self and when you enhance your pure self, so is your contribution to **all** more pure.*
You are here to exist by pure means.

Souls

Souls are here, but we do not see them.
Souls are easier to feel.
We typically cannot see or hear spirits.

Spiritual Visitations

Visits happen all the time.
During sleep, we are more available.
It's all by way of your hand.
You determine what you are ready and available for.

Dane Boggs

You get what you need and what you are ready for.
This keeps it true.
It does not need to be on a conscious level.
It does not need to pass through those particular filters.
Do not limit yourself with the conscious mind.
Place yourself in a ready position.
That availability creates the access.
Visitations are always possible.

Spirituality

We are spiritual beings.
It is instinctive to be drawn to our spirituality.
It's part of our essence.
Everything one does has a component of spirituality.

Splatter

There is no need to splatter yourself all over the place.
Your head can push you beyond what is balanced.
Trust your own assessment and evaluation as to what seems right and appropriate
*   for you.*
It's okay to share yourself, just don't splatter yourself.
Your assessment is the one that matters the most.

Spontaneity

Be in the moment and take things on the fly.
One can deal with it as it comes.
Being spontaneous creates a standing that is stronger and more whole.
Travel often involves plans and not spontaneity.
Expand the perception of what is acceptable.

Stimulates

Stimulants create a tendency for one to overextend oneself.
They can mask one's tendency to rest.
Awareness and clarity of self are kept at bay.

A false sense is created.
It takes time to restore the balance.

Strength

Sometimes humans feel vulnerable.
Some people prefer to be weak.
Remind oneself of one's strength.
You are greater than any challenge that comes your way.
Nothing is given or occurs in one's life that is bigger or more powerful than one's ability to survive and excel.

Student

The most powerful aspect of the student is the student's openness and willingness to learn.

Suicide

Suicide often is predicated by despondency.
If one's passage is routed by way of despondency, it is almost always premature.

Suicide

Suicide often creates remorse and disappointment later for the soul.

Support

Everyone has their own source of support, assistance, guidance, and direction.
They support you in the way you intended for yourself.
They support your fruition.
It is a fellowship.
Everything they are is what you need.
Everything you are is what they need.
All matches are made in heaven.
The system is very efficient.
There is always something to share and gain.
There is mutual and equal benefit.

Surrendering

*Entrust yourself to **all**.*
*Give yourself over to **all**.*
Mold me, shape me, and guide me.
Give yourself back.
This is the process of conjoining all. Join with the oneness.
It's surrendering.
This will expand one's possibilities beyond one's own capacities.

Survival

Survival is a human thing.
The nature of humanness is to cling to life.
It's natural and instinctive.
It doesn't have to be an attachment.
Attachment to life is not the most respectful thing one can do, but it is
*   understandable.*
Human perspectives are limited.
Death is part of the life cycle.
It's not the worst thing that can happen.
We are not more important than the animals and nature.

Synchronicity

Proper timing for all is a production.
It's hard to grasp for humans.
Everything is exactly as it needs to be.
Synchronicity exists in every moment.
It's constant and common.
It's bigger than our minds can comprehend.
Our awareness is not necessary.
Divine moments are not restricted to the things we understand, appreciate, or
*   enjoy.*
Everything is as it needs to be, whether it is comfortable or not.
Humans see historical, present, and future.
All that is, is beyond all that.
It's not directional or planned out.

There are no words to explain how it is different.
All is as it needs to be.

Synchronicity

Whenever things are appropriate, circumstances cannot interfere with them.
You can be late, and if it is appropriate, it will all work out.
Synchronicity can also keep you from things that are not appropriate.
There is always a bigger picture.

Synchronized

The universe is synchronized all the time.
Every moment.
There's magic and connection all the time.
This too shall pass.
Everything that you are feeling right now will be behind you at some point.
Sometimes life goes exactly as you like.
Don't hold on to it too tight because it will change.
Life is always changing.
Don't become too attached.
Be in the flow.

Take the Ride

Change is constant.
Resistance to change can be painful.
Take the ride.

Take Your Time

Be in the moment as thoroughly, fully, and completely as you are capable.
Give every place that you are your attentiveness, acknowledging its value and
    significance.
Give whatever you are doing your full focus.
It gives homage to all.
Give it its proper due.
Experience where you are and everything it offers.

It alleviates the human tendency to assess and judge by way of value or
importance.

Template

Each soul has a template for each life.
Some overcome the template and decide to stay longer.
Due to physical longevity, more people are willing to stay and help.
Walk-ins can occur where another soul takes over a body that has died but is
still good.
Sometimes a personality change is noticed.
Some souls want to bypass infancy and childhood.
All of this is managed by the divine.
You cannot be against the divine.

The Endgame

The human experience is about individuality and independence.
The endgame is to recognize that all that appears to be separate is not.
There is nothing separate.
Leaving behind what is without significance, know that all is significant.
Consider that **all is one**.
Nothing happens unless the whole benefits.
Inside of you, you know all.
The more embracing you are of yourself, the closer you are to God.

Thoughts

Your imaginings soon become memories.
Once you imagine something, it is a reality and becomes a memory.
Be conscious of your thoughts.

Tools

Tools work for humans.
Humans connect to the truth with tools.
Tools are not the gift but access to the gift.
God is always available.

True for You

Develop the ability to pick and choose.
In your society, it seems to be all or nothing.
Retain your own sense of power in the midst of whatever you are experiencing.
Attend and attune to your own and what you clearly resonant with.
It's how we each position ourselves.
Obtain a pure and defined position with yourself.
There are places for you to be that benefit from your presence.
There are places where you benefit and circumstances that contain both.
If you abide by what is true for you, you will always find yourself where you
*   need to be.*
Validate your own sense of personal truth.
What is yours is to be most embraced and held by you.

Trust

What you see is just.
Everything that occurs is just.
Trust is valuable in human living.
Trust now and have peace.
Hindsight will be valuable later.
Clarity will come later.
Accept and find peace.

Truth

Truth is to be found by way of personal resonation.
When you hear your truth, you will resonate with it.
It has to do with everyone's unique and varying positions.

Unique

There is nothing or no one like you or that replicates you.
The form of you is unique.
There is room to grow and expand.
There are so many different possibilities—endless possibilities.

Dane Boggs

Usefulness

There are different levels of usefulness.
When things are no longer useful, they become extinct.
They conclude and become complete.
It's all divinely regulated.

Vacancies

Often we human beings live our entire lives with vacancies.
This is not necessary.
One word or gesture can fill the need or want that we lacked as children.
Everything you change in the past has a ripple effect into the future.
What did you need or want as a child and did not get?
Repair and restructure your childhood self.

Vibration and Consciousness

A higher vibration is more important than conscious awareness.
Being conscious is not a prerequisite for a higher vibration.
The consciousness of our planet is higher now than at any other time.
There's always an opportunity for more.
You are much more than your consciousness.

Volunteer

Every life is to be seen as its own unique opportunity.
Everyone here is a volunteer.
Whatever the life experience, whatever the life circumstances, everyone volunteered.

We Are Needed

Where we are is where we are needed.
Who we are makes a difference.

What Is

Wrap your mind around things in a nonintellectual way.

*Give yourself the opportunity to accept **what is**.*
*Acceptance of **what is** creates peace and comfort.*

Whims

Your whims need no justification.
Whims and inclinations are opportunistic; they come for a reason.
They are soul oriented.
You need not know what the reason is or whether your award is apparent or
*   unapparent.*

Will and Intention

Recognize your capacity and broadness in any given situation.
The portion that is used is determined by one's will and intention.
Will and intention are behind one's growth and expansion.
If you bring broader will and intention into varying circumstances, you will
*   be more comfortable and balanced.*

Willingness and Surrender

Willingness creates the opportunity for transformation.
Willingness is the same as surrender.
Great magnificence can be offered, but one must be in the proper position.

Wishing

Wishing is important.
Expand your mind and heart into fancy.
Utilize the energy of all to support unimaginable headings.
On the wings of a dove, anything is possible.
Participate at a level beyond boundaries.
Release limitations.

Without Attachment

Approach an existence without attachment.
This will make room for your heavenly essence.

Dane Boggs

Writing

Writing takes one to a deeper level.
It's like pulling the curtain back.
It's revealing.
It's an in-depth expression of one's internal nature.
Writing can engage the intellect, but it does not have to be based in the intellect;
    just let it emerge.
Creative allowance combined with intellect is fuller, richer, and more revealing.

IVO SPEAKS TO REIKI PRACTICTIONERS

Feel free to skip this section if you are not a Reiki practitioner. This section contains information for those who specialize in energy work. Please give yourself the time you need to understand and digest this material. Let Ivo's words guide you when you treat yourself and others. Ask for assistance and blessings. Maintain energetic definition and purity. Grounding practices will increase your vibration and expansion. Both of these will increase your ability to transfer light. Energetic cleansing is required before and after each session. Avoid energetic deletion of self. Share the light and become one with All That Is.

Alone

If you feel alone, open your crown chakra to God's divine light.

Ascension

Remember the whole of you is not your body.
The higher self is an aspect of you that is not held in the body.
Ascension is extending and expanding the vibration of your essence while
*   maintaining a connection to the physical body.*
Ascension used to occur when bodies were no longer living, now some physical
*   bodies are stretching themselves to hold that higher vibration.*
This in turn raises the vibration of the planet.
This is progress for the human species.

Attunements

*Reiki masters attune us to **all**.*

The attunement to **all** is the intention and purpose, acknowledging oneself
   as **all**.
It reminds us of **all** we are and **all** we know.
That's the resonation.

Balance

You can maintain balance in the midst of anything.
Do the chakra weave to keep yourself balanced.
You have the tools available.
It is a choice.
Balance comes from many places.

Balance

What balanced one in the past may not in the future.
Illnesses, tragedies, and heartaches can come from imbalances.
Distractions can cause an imbalance.
Get rid of distractions.
Balance delivers the soul and **all that is** to the world.

Balance and Lift

Balance and lift within allows you to hold your own and be your own in a
   divine capacity.
There is no effort or force, just allowance.
We are ever changing and ever moving.
We are in constant flux.

Blockages

Energy blockages can be physical, mental, emotional, or spiritual.
They can be cleared, released, or reclaimed.
Any energy that is not your own is unwanted energy.
Unwanted energy may be honorable but is misguided.

Capacity

One is less likely to be intimidated by other energetic resources, people, places,
*   or things when one's energy shifts to a higher capacity.*

Capacity and Docking

Capacity has nothing to do with the size and shape of the physical body.
It is not uncommon for the capacity of the body to be less than the capacity of
*   the soul.*
It is possible to bring more of the soul into the body.
It's a docking process.
This can be a trying process.
Rest if you feel tired.
One's needs may not make sense.
Passivity is part of the docking process.
Get ready.
Prepare for the event.
Experience the event.
Adjust to the event.
This is very consuming.
This dynamic is out of the ordinary.
It is less common.
This supports the purity of one's standing.
Typically this is a rarity, but at this current time, it is more frequent.
We are talking about the amount of soul one's body functions with.
One's progression allows the body to hold more of one's soul or essence.
This is a reflection of humankind's progression.

Challenge

Who you are and who you can become is greater than any challenge.
Call all of yourself to your center.
*Call yourself and the resource of **all that is**.*
This will enable you to be more balanced and centered.
Every step you take enhances your capacity.

Choices

When you put energy into something that is aligned, the feedback is great.
Find a way to feed yourself.
What parts are not being fed?
It's not about what you are doing but what you are not doing.

Conveyance

When you are present and current with self, you are present and current
*   with all.*
Being in your own purely supports the purity of your offering.
Say what you need to say.
Everyone will hear what they need to hear.
Don't get distracted by what is outside you.
Recognize that what others hear may not be what you said at all.
What everyone gets from it is his or her own.
You are not in charge of what others hear.

Definition

Sometimes outside sources can dilute your essence.
Be deliberate in what you invite in.
Encapsulate yourself for energetic definition.
Holding one's own is of the upmost importance.

Definition

It is important to define one's energy.
There are so many different people, dynamics, and components.
Avoid the energetic debris of others.
It is easy to become externally distracted and accessible.
Stay in a position and place that is right for you.
This will help you retain your vitality and energetic nature.
Sustain yourself and your energetic reservoirs.

Deletion

When you think about something too much, it goes to your head.

Energy leaves your body.
It leaves your immune system defenseless, which can create a sense of imbalance.
You tire more easily, and your physical resistance will wane.
Do not delete yourself with excessive thinking.

Docking

When you die, the things you learned in that life and afterlife promote an
opportunity to hold a greater capacity for the soul.
Typically the downloading of the soul occurs with the new body.
Docking gives one the opportunity to invite more of the soul on board during
one's current life.
It is encouraged on earth at this time.
One can exist at a fuller capacity.
Struggles and difficulties will not seem so when the docking is complete.
One will recognize a new ease.
This represents an advancement of humankind and an opportunity for
expansion in the universe.
It's an earthly dynamic that supports something much greater.
*Docking creates a profitable and effective standing in the world for **all**.*
*It's an offering for **all**.*

Docking

Expansion is a necessary prerequisite to docking.
Docking then leads to more expansion.

Energetic Body

Be aware of your energetic body.
Be aware of your core.
Illuminate yourself at the core level.
Create energetic distinction and definition.
Use a filter.
Fluff yourself.
Fill your reservoir.
Be a golden egg.

Energetic Compression and Expansion

Energetic compression and expansion can occur at the same time.
All of us are expanding, some at a faster pace, some at a level pace.
Often we compress energetically and create a buffer for ourselves.
One can retract one's energy to create a clear awareness of oneself in the midst
of that which is new and broad and sometimes overwhelming.
This compression of energy can be useful.
Growing evokes expansion.
Curiosity when traveling can bump up expansion.
Expansion creates congestion when it comes up against your compression.
It is important to re-assimilate to your natural state of being.

Energetic Debris

Off-loading of energetic debris is necessary—yours and that of others.
Sometimes an exchange of energy is part of intimacy.
That is acceptable.
It still requires release, cleansing, and disposal.

Energetic Sensitivity

It's not about protection.
An increase in one's energetic sensitivity can create vulnerability.
Practice definition and intention in everyday moments.
Create and sustain an energetic perimeter.
This will maintain one's purity and clarity.
The more pure one's standing, the greater one's effect.
Utilize oneself at optimum levels.
Hold your own in this world.
Don't be a leaf blowing in the wind.
Sustain your boundaries.
Claim your own.

Energy

Everything is energy.
Make sure your energy is contained and pure.
Do not compromise your personal boundaries.

Do not carry around other people's stuff.
Do not dissipate energy to the past or future.
When you feel safe and secure and pure, you will deliver that which is even
more profound.

Energy

Everything is comprised of energy.
There is nothing that is not energy.
Everything in existence is energy, whether tangible or not—a word, a thought,
an object, or an action.
Everything in the physical world vibrates approximately the same.
Reiki energy is soul energy.
Earth energy is body energy.
Both are divine and pure.

Energy

There is no such thing as good or bad energy.
Stay clear of these labels.
Use the terms balance and out of balance.

Energy

Different areas of the country have different energy.
Everything that has been in place contributes to the energy.
The place, people, and plants contribute to the energy.

Giving Reiki

Quietness invites Reiki receptivity.
When giving Reiki, it is very important to keep your emotions out of it.
Maintain a position of divine purity.
Reiki offerings have no success or failure.
Step into the flow, and you will participate with the divine.
A position of giving and sharing can bring peace, contentment, and neutrality.

Dane Boggs

God

God is all.
There is nothing that is not God.

Grounding

Walking on the earth can be very grounding.
Sense and feel the contact.
Yoga can be very grounding.
Hold earth energy consistently for stabilization.
The activity of yoga and Qigong are very grounding.
Grounding provides stability with regard to places, people, and things that are not yours.

Grounding

Grounding supports extension of self—the soul.
The soul can reach further if the body is grounded.
The soul wants to be assured that the connection will not be severed.
Grounding is about holding one's own and maintaining truth and stability.
Grounding increases the reach of one's vibration and is very important in Reiki.
This will support further expansion.

Grounding

It is important to ground oneself when doing energy work.
Because we are human, there will be a physical effect.
An awareness can be lacking with a purely energetic long-distance treatment.
Grounding allows one to support a balanced position while retaining a physical body.
It is a necessity while in a physical body.
Grounding supports further expansion.
Grounding comes to us by intention.

Grounding and Transcending

Grounding is an important component of one's transcending.
Grounding is a great advantage.

Ground oneself with a chakra weave and conscious intent.
Inhale and exhale the earth's energy.
Envision the light of God connecting one to the core of the earth.
When one is secure and stable on this earth, the soul and Reiki energy can extend beyond.
This promotes stability for one and one's offering.
This enhances Reiki.
Grounding will extend your vibrational energy.
Don't restrict yourself by failing to ground yourself.
Support your expansion by grounding.
The transcending process can make one out of sorts.
Some things and people will not resonant with one as one transcends.
Don't hold yourself to a place that is unnecessary, undesired, or inappropriate for you.
Keep your eyes open on all levels.
Be educated and prepared.
Don't go blindly.
Create efficient proficiency.
Transcendence is a continuing process.
Recognize your accomplishments.

Guides

Guides can show you how to turn up the intensity of your light.

Illuminada

Do not let what someone else says or does hold you down.
Leave it in the past.
Say "Illuminada" and rise above.
Rise above and experience purity.
Practice purity of heart and mind.
This allows one to hold one's position.
People with special intellectual and spiritual enlightenment possess illuminada.

Input and Output

Keep a watchful eye on energetic input and output.

Participate as is appropriate.
Be self-attentive.
Input is what you bring in.
Output is what you convey.
We are limited by our physical capacities.

Input and Output

Do not overextend oneself.
Overextension will cause one's vitality to wane.
Giving Reiki is output.
One must not let one's output be greater than one's input.
Being in the moment fills one up.

Integration

Integrate your spirit into your human existence.
Bring the wholeness of your existence into your living.
Create a whole standing in your world.

Intellect

Intellect uses logic, rationality, and reason.
Intellect uses more energy.
Intuition is acceptance.
Intuition uses less energy.

Knowing

Knowing can be downloaded on an innate and internal level by guides.
Things will be more clear and focused.
A better sense of clarity will prevail.
You will have a more magnanimous and broader perspective.
*You will have an ability to experience **all that is**.*
*Work with **all that is** rather than separately from it.*
Utilize your experience and surroundings in a manner that supports you.

Long-Distance Attunements

Long-distance attunements work.
Energy is not restricted by physical boundaries.
Energy is energy.
Long-distance attunements are not secondary, just different.
One is not any better than the other.

Long-Distance Reiki

Sending Reiki to more than one person at a time is not diminished.
It is not contained by space.
How it is conveyed is unique to each individual.
One's intention is most important.
Intention is not limited by measurement and containment.
Share and align with the divine.
It is not limited or contained.
Be loose with it.
Why restrict?
***All that is**, is beyond capacity.*

Moon

The moon can affect the amount of energy one absorbs during Reiki.

Offering

With Reiki, one creates an offering.
Do not develop any attachments to offerings.
Do not create attachments by appearances, assumptions, or individual perceptions.
Not everyone is ready to embark on this journey.
Where each person is, what his or her own process is, what he or she is ready for, and what his or her capacity is will vary greatly.
Recognize the divine position they hold.
Treatments may be profound to one and insignificant to another.
Reiki is always divine, but it can look different each time.

Dane Boggs

Overexertion

Overexertion is not necessarily a physical thing; it can be energetic.
Overexertion compromises balance.
It is a moving line.
Create a keen perception.
Be with yourself in an appropriate manner.

Permission

It's important to be granted permission for giving Reiki.
Once you get permission, it is proper.
Get permission from the physical body or soul.
It is more effective if you invoke participation on one or both levels.

Pooling of Energy

When you are still for a long time, there is a pooling of energy.
The lack of physical movement at night can create stiffness.
If spiritual activity is prominent, there is a tendency for all else to be settled.
If you are out of your body more and moving around spiritually, it leaves the body more sedentary energetically.
The more active the soul is at night, the more sedentary the body.
The soul is not being required to operate and maintain the body.
Activity can occur, such as accomplishing, achieving, learning, good deeds, and good works.
Energy tends to pool due to lack of movement.
Gentle, encouraging activity, movements, and fluidity are most appreciated by the body in the morning.

Position and Capacity

Perception of the world is a reflection of one's position and capacity.
Personal capacity precedes everything one does.
The channel between the heart and head must be open to operate at a higher position.
Sustaining an investment of divine intention allows one to continue on a productive path.
One's position, desire, and willingness bring pure knowledge into consciousness.

This transfers innate knowing into intellectual capacity.
This must be done from a place of balance.
You can never unlearn something.
One cannot go backward.
One cannot be less.
One cannot revert.
All progression is eternal.

Power

The present moment is the place of greatest power.

Reiki

Reiki is an offering from God.
Reiki knows no bounds.
The universe decides what happens with Reiki treatments.
The universe decides what is in the best interest of all.
Reiki aligns the soul and body.
It deepens the connection between the soul and body.
*Reiki attunes us with **all that is**.*

Reiki

Whatever happens with a Reiki treatment is exactly what is supposed to happen.
Whatever happens is absolutely perfect for the time.
What happens is divine.
Do not get caught up in effectiveness and attachment.
Make sure blessings and cleansings happen every time after you give Reiki.

Reiki

The universe decides what happens with Reiki treatments.
The universe decides what is in the best interest of all.
Sometimes a full flow is of benefit.
Sometimes a partial flow is of benefit.
Sometimes no flow is of benefit.

Dane Boggs

Reiki

There is always benefit from a treatment.
Sometimes it is consciously known and sometimes not.
Make sure you do a backward spiral at the end of your Reiki session.
This keeps your energy and the receiver's energy separate.
Everyone is more pure and clear.

Reiki

Remain unattached when giving Reiki.
One's best position is to be neutral.
Participate from a place of pure mind and heart.
That is how one creates the greatest effect.
Give honor and respect.
Respect the whole.
Every situation and person is unique.
Being present and lost in the moment is okay.
Being at rest is okay.
Being elsewhere is a distraction and is not okay.

Reiki

Energetic treatments are not confined by logic, rationality, or reason.
When one makes oneself available, what is needed occurs.
Reiki goes out through every part and cell of the body.

Reiki

Amazing things can happen when you are open and without attachment.
Amazing things can happen when you garner that position.
It increases the possibilities tenfold.

Reiki

With Reiki, intention is everything.
Don't get caught up in logistics.

Reiki

Reiki nourishes the body and soul.
The soul and the body are one.
The soul and body benefit from Reiki.
The soul benefits from the restoration process because it is part of the whole.
The soul does not need Reiki, but it benefits from the symmetry, balance, and
*   unity it creates.*
The soul does not lack, but it is part of the body, so it benefits.
More ease and unity come from Reiki.

Reiki

When giving Reiki to others, do not ask for evidence of value.
Avoid any insistence on your part.
Do not attach to any one picture or dynamic.
What they do with Reiki is of their choosing.

Reiki

One cannot share Reiki if one possesses a need for it.

Reiki

Reiki can support departure.

Reiki

Reiki is a union of two coming together.
It's like a partnership, giving and receiving jointly.
Mutual participation creates a union, utilizing the connection in an
*   intention way.*
Humanness is demonstrated.
God, the energy of all, is the avenue.

Reiki

Some of us have specific Reiki guides.
*Some of us work from the collective **all**.*

Reiki Absorption

So much of the absorption has to do with proper preparation and readiness.
It is not a conscious process.
What you need to know in a conscious way always finds its way there.
Absorption must be needed and possible.
*Readiness must be in conjunction with **all**.*
Changes will not occur if it inhibits the growth process.
It is quite complex.

Reiki Energy

Reiki energy does not work around volume.
Volume is a human term.
It's not predicated by size and volume.
It cannot be contained.
It can be defined by purity.
The purity of your intention supports the offering.

Sacred Geometry

You must have an awareness that shapes have energy.
No shape is better than another.
Shapes can be used to support one's standing.
Shapes can anchor one to create a personal and functional symmetry with one's
*   surroundings.*

Self-Reiki

When doing self-Reiki, you cannot force or push something that is inappropriate.
You cannot override God.

Self-Reiki

Envision light coming into your body for self-healing.

Self-Reiki

With self-Reiki, do not create unnecessary displeasure.

There is no reason to take yourself to a place of discomfort.
It doesn't take you any further in the healing process.
When the body feels pain, it feels small.
Do not let pain challenge your vitality and balance.
Promote Reiki to a place that is not painful.
There is a point where pain becomes terror.
The body ceases to accept the offering.
The body will not accept more than it can use.
The body starts to defend itself against the pain.
No damage is done.
You cannot do too much self-Reiki.
When you work with yourself, you have the experience of both sides.
This allows you to be a better practitioner.

Sensitivity

An increase in one's sensitivity saves one from mistreating oneself.

Sensitivity

When you grow, part of your growth is an increase in vibration.
The increase in vibration can be an aspect of greater sensitivity.
Sensitivity can be inconvenient at times.
Overall it is a plus.

Separation

Acknowledge no separation.
We have a physical body, we are individuals, and we have specific bodies and
*   humanness, but that is not who we are.*
We are distinct and one at the same time.

Shell and Shift

The shell is an energetic dynamic that comes before renewal, like a snake losing
*   its skin.*
It is a shift that will lend itself to never being the same again.
Vulnerability can occur afterward.

It can create a lift.
Behold and cherish this new standing.
It will have different needs and desires.
Give yourself the proper opportunity to reveal yourself.
Stay self-aware.
Be current with yourself.
This will promote the reinforcement of the shift.

Soul

Soul momentum is always forward.
It may be slow, but it never ceases.
It can't go backward.

Subleavient

Taking that which is below and underneath.
Bring it up the surface and make use of it.
That can create balance.
Resources are brought to the surface.
There are treasure troves that can be accessed.
When you come to this body, sometimes life and living are placed in a clear-cut manner, but a lot remains optional that you can access and utilize by way of discretion.
This resource is plentiful and abundant.
Very rarely do we as human beings come to the end of it.
Usually if we come to the end of all that is as a resource, it's departure time.

Vibration

The goal is to increase your vibration.
Incorporate more of the soul into the physical body.
Grounding is stabilization.
Say the word grounding.
Be with earth.
Walk on the earth.
Meditation and prayer create a higher vibration.

Some people get very high in vibration when they meditate.
Drugs and alcohol lower one's vibration.

Vibration

Everything has its own vibration.
Find what resonates with you.
Soul expansion is heightened when the body experiences expansion.
Yoga and Qigong are moving meditations.
Doing both is a physical and spiritual experience.
You are both a human being and a spiritual being.

Vibration

Energy is vibration.
Typically the body's energy is at a lower vibration.
The soul's energy is a higher vibration.
When the two come together, they normally meet in the middle.
For the soul to be connected and contained to a body, the vibration has to be
*   lowered.*
Meditation raises one's vibration.
We can attune to each other's vibration as well as a shared universal vibration.
All people are in a different level of progression with their energy bodies.

Wind

Wind scatters energy.
Watch out for ill effects, especially if one's energy is not well contained.
Defining one's energetic body and parameters will help reduce the effects of
*   wind.*

SUMMARY

Two diseases—Huntington's and Lyme—the departure of my dog, and my Reiki awakening enabled me to accept Ivo as a teacher of *truth*. We are here to learn and grow, to further ourselves, and to become enlightened. The endgame is a planet of enlightened souls. Listen to Ivo's words of wisdom, compassion, and love. Find more peace and comfort. Let your divinity shine forth. We do not need to suffer as we do. Exercise your free will. Play an active role in your life. You are responsible for your thoughts, feelings, and actions. Become a mature, enlightened soul.

Recognize that all that appears to be separate is not. There is nothing separate. We are *all one*. You are *all that is*.

Below are some *Questions for You* to ponder. See where my questions lead you. What doors do they open?

The *Remember the Basics* list comes from Ivo. Use the list to see the world more clearly.

The *Dos—Thou Shall* list comes from Ivo. Put your energy and effort into this list. Increase your capacity, and bring more of your soul into your body. Make sure your thoughts, feelings, and actions move you closer to God.

The *Do Nots—Thou Shalt Not* list comes from Ivo and is just as important. Don't do anything that dulls your shine.

The *Enlightenment Formula* represents one path to greater enlightenment. There are many paths for this unfolding. It does not look one way. Enlightenment is a process, not a destination.

Meditation connects you to the divine. Do this to stay balanced and centered.

The practice of the *Daily Tips* will create more comfort, peace, and bliss in your life.

QUESTIONS FOR YOU . . .

Why are you here?
Do you believe in God?
Do you have a soul?
Do you practice self-awareness?
Are you dedicated to the self?
Is the self the same as God?
What do you do to stay balanced, centered, and grounded?
How do you express your divinity?
How do you connect to God?
Do you believe in reincarnation?
Do you have a contract to fulfill in this life?
What would you like to release?
Do you control your thoughts, feeling, and actions?
Do you look at everything as an opportunity to learn and grow?
Do you exercise your free will to move closer to God?
What happens when and after you die?

REMEMBER THE BASICS . . .

*There is a **God**.*
We are all divine.
Our souls are eternal.
Our souls enter the body when we are born.
Our souls leave the body when we die.
We are here to learn and grow.
We are here to further ourselves.
We are here to become advanced souls.

Dane Boggs

We are here to let our divinity shine forth.
We are here to become enlightened beings.

We are not separate.
There is nothing separate.
We only think we are separate.
*We are **all one**.*
*You are **all that is**.*

There is more than meets the eye.
Nothing happens unless the whole benefits.
Whatever you see is just.
Everything that occurs is just.
Trust now and have peace.
Clarity will come later.

Divine purity is the result of being free and clear.

*Experience **oneness** with **all** and within yourself.*

*Rooting within connects one to **all that is**.*

*Inside you, you know **all**.*

Fatigue is anything that doesn't nourish the soul.

Change is constant.
Resistance to change creates pain.
Acceptance lessens pain.

Everything is energy.

We create for ourselves that which best supports our divine unfolding.
For some it is pain.
For others it is camaraderie, support, and encouragement.
It comes in varying forms to support our furthering.

The universe decides what happens with Reiki treatments.
The universe decides what is in the best interest of all.

Grounding increases one's vibration.
Grounding supports the expansion of the soul.

You are always safe.
When you die, you know you are safe.

When people die, they do not stay that age or in that place.
Don't get stuck to something that no longer exists.
The relationship is not severed when the body dies.
The relationship continues.
The more healing your heart is capable of, the more freedom the departed one gets.

The soul chooses the body it occupies, and the divine confirms.

Suicide often creates remorse and disappointment later for the soul.

Do not discount any of your journey.
The path is different for all of us.
It's a process.

*God is **all**.*
There is nothing that is not God.

We are never sure of another's position.
We only know our own.

Our state of being is pure.

Safety, security, and stability are inward based.

Everyone is part of everyone.
There is no separation.
Oneness reigns.

Dane Boggs

The earth is not the center of it all.

Attunements are a divine rite.

Who you are makes a difference.
Where you are is where you are needed.

You have everything you need.

Every step you take enhances your capacity.

See the beauty and profoundness of existence.

Everyone has their own source of support, assistance, guidance, and direction.
God is always available.

Heaven is soulful continence.
Hell is soulful disappointment.

Each soul has a template for each life.

You know everything already.
You are universal knowledge.

Comfort requires a consistent process of regarding self well.

*The soul is the reference for **all**.*

***All** is divine.*

*Balance delivers the soul and **all that is** to the world.*

Happiness is our essence.

Be in the flow with endless possibilities.
Release expectations.

All progression is eternal.

No place is a disadvantage.
One is greater than any challenge that comes one's way.

Any energy that is not your own is unwanted energy.

We are spiritual beings.

All is significant.
You can't help but include yourself in it.

Willingness creates the opportunity for transformation.

Grounding supports further expansion.

Each part of you is vital, significant, and important.

Nothing is outside of God.

We are not more important than the animals and nature.

No one else can determine your balance.

There's always a bigger picture.

You are here to exist by way of pure means.

All life is sacred.

*Acceptance of **what is** creates peace and comfort.*

Earth is a place where great soul advancement can occur.

Life is a powerful and complex existence.

Laughter can create cleansing, purification, and divine expressions.
Laughter is a pure expression of self.

Dane Boggs

Favor yourself.

Everyone here is a volunteer.

Any human projection is limited as to what it's all about.
The human mind does not have the capacity or ability to comprehend it.
There are no original thoughts.

Be in the moment as thoroughly, fully, and completely as you are capable.
Give whatever you are doing your full focus.
It gives homage to all.

Remember, everything you are and have been is within.
Remember, when your position to yourself changes your position to all changes.

Departure is between one's soul and God.
Each departure is fit for one's needs and goals.

Enlightenment is not a destination; it's a process.
Enlightenment doesn't look one way.
All different forms of unfolding are available.

Religions are principles and practices that allow each to find their way to God.

God is within you.
***All that is**, is within you.*
It's all self-possessed.

You are a radiant being of light.

Remember, there is always a bigger picture.

Karma is always balancing.

Each has their own method of passage.

Your change affects and influences all.

Everything you are contributes to everything that is.
Human living comes with stressors.
You get to choose your position in how you respond.

The personal self and the whole are not separate.

The vibration of all on earth is greater than in the past.

It's almost impossible to avoid collecting karmic debt.
It's part of living.

Allow yourself feel and know the beauty and perfection of this existence.
It's a simple pleasure.
Recognize as many moments as you can as often as you can.

The mind has a limited capacity.
The mind is a conceptual mind.
Existence is not a concept.

Independent growth and development are important, but it means nothing without supporting all.
It's about wholeness.
It's about oneness!

Choose a place that is comfortable for you because it is appropriate, not a place that is comfortable because it is familiar.

Remember to always honor, trust, and follow your heart.

Muscle testing is a great tool for self-support.

Overextension and overexertion can make being here less appealing.

Frequency treatments are offerings and contribution for others.
The offering is there to support the vibrational change or not.
Some will choose to create a change, and some will not.

All is energy.
All is vibration.
All is varying levels of vibration.
Everything is influenced by energy.

We cannot put God into conceptual terms.
As humans that's what we like to do.

God is not a concept.
All *at its core is pure.*
All is of God.

Acknowledge oneself as all.
All is as it needs to be.
All is just.
All is of balance.
All is divine.
All is of God.

DOS — THOU SHALL

Entrust yourself to **all.**
Give yourself to **all.**
Surrender.
Become one with **all.**
Practice purity of heart.
Be your pure self.
Embrace and acknowledge your shine.
Maintain energetic purity and definition.
Sustain your energetic reservoirs.
Maintain personal and energetic balance.
Focus on all that is grand.
See the profoundness and beauty of existence.
See the beauty and perfection of **all.**
Let your marriage be a union that is valid, strong, true, and supportive of each other.
Let your marriage be a joyful acceptance of each other's differences.

Allow yourself to soar and be utilized as a tool of God.
Honor the bravery of each soul.
Acknowledge the evolution of your existence.
Hold a position that is grounded and dedicated to self.
Remain supportive, encouraging, and comforting of yourself all the days of your life.
Practice gratitude.
Remember to always honor, trust and follow your heart.

DO NOTS—THOU SHALT NOT

Do not scorn.
Do not judge others.
Do not berate or judge yourself.
Do not carry other people's stuff.
Do not get distracted by the intentions, situations, and processes of others.
Do not fashion yourself after another.
Do not discount any of your journey.
Do not get stuck to something that no longer exists.
Do not involve yourself outwardly in a nonbalanced way.
Do not compromise your energetic boundaries.
Do not let your energetic output be greater than your input.
Do not become attached to any particular pattern or system.
Do not limit yourself with the conscious mind.
Do not let go of your covenant relationship with self.
Do not hold yourself to a place that is unnecessary, undesired, or inappropriate.
Do not let fear direct your life.

ENLIGHTENMENT FORMULA

$$SA + DS = > PEB + G = > VE = > DP = > E$$

Self-Awareness + Dedication to Self = > Personal and Energetic Balance + Grounding = > Vibration and Expansion = > Docking Possibilities = > Enlightenment

My path to greater enlightenment is shown above. Your path will be unique to you. Ivo said, *"Enlightenment is a process, not a destination. It's what occurs as the soul grows and expands. Enlightenment doesn't look one way. The process is unique and distinct for each person. There are many dynamics available for this unfolding."*

Self-awareness is knowing that God resides within you. Ivo said, *"God is within you. All that is, is within you. It's all self-possessed."*

Dedication to self from a place of self-awareness promotes greater personal and energetic balance. Ivo said, *"Create a trusting, supportive, and valid relationship with self. Be dedicated and devoted to yourself. This will provide you with a great sense of security, safety, and stability. Have a profound relationship with self. This relationship can be very effective and valuable."*

Balance delivers the soul and *All That Is* to the world. Your divine offering comes from a place of balance. Ivo said, *"The more balance one retains, the greater one's ability and offering. Each of us is a resource of balance. This contributes to the balance of* **all***. When you are in a place of balance, everything benefits. One can bring more balance to whatever imbalance is occurring. A huge part of this is one's ability to be more fluid. What balanced one in the past may not in the future. No one else can determine your balance."* Do whatever it takes to stay balanced, centered, and grounded.

Ivo said, *"Grounding supports the extension of the self—the soul. Grounding supports further expansion and one's transcending. Grounding is stabilizing. Grounding allows one to support a balanced position while retaining a physical body. Grounding is a necessity while in the physical body. Grounding comes to us by conscious intent. Say the word grounding. Do the chakra weave. Walk on the earth."* Feel yourself connected to the center of earth. Grounding practices increase your personal vibration and expansion.

Ivo said, *"The goal is to increase your vibration. A higher vibration is more important than conscious awareness. Being conscious is not a prerequisite for a higher vibration. Expansion is a prerequisite for docking. Docking leads to more expansion. Docking gives one the opportunity to invite more of the soul on board during one's current life."* The docking process is available for *all*. Ivo said, *"This process is becoming more and more common. Typically this is a rarity, but at this current time, it is happening more frequently. This is a reflection of humankind's progression. Willingness creates the opportunity for surrender. This will expand one's possibilities beyond one's own capacities."* Your willingness, openness, and surrender are an integral part of this docking process.

"Some souls are now creating ascension while in the physical body. Ascension is what happens after the soul leaves the physical body. Souls are now inhabiting the planet that have the ability to ascend and maintain presence in the physical body. This is progress for the human species. Human bodies are not made for ascension, to transcend without leaving the body behind, where the body accompanies the soul and energy on its journey. Evolved souls are choosing to return to earth with this intention of creating ascension and maintaining the physical body simultaneously—to alter and change the vibration of the soul beyond what is typical in the physical world. Ascension here on earth can assist us all and is a good thing. People are staying where before they left, sharing that it can be done and guiding others in the same possibilities. It's occurring and is in existence. The more success there is, the more there can be. Ascension can happen again and again."

Ivo said, *"Perception of the world is a reflection of one's position and capacity. We are never sure of another's position. We only know our own. It is best if unfair comparisons are avoided between people. Personal capacity precedes everything one does. Sustaining an investment of divine intention allows one to continue on a productive path. Will and intention are behind one's growth and expansion. One's position, desire, and willingness bring pure knowledge into consciousness. This transfers innate knowing into intellectual capacity. This must be done from a place of balance. All progression is eternal."*

You can become more enlightened. You can have more peace and comfort in your life. You can move toward greater personal and energetic balance. Your struggles and difficulties can be less. Exercise your free will. You are so much more than your body. You are an eternal, radiant being of light. Know this to be true.

Ask yourself this question: *What can I do at this moment to create greater balance in my life?* Ivo said, *"The most powerful moment in your life is **now**."* Ask yourself, "What thoughts and actions do I need to exercise at this moment to be more balanced?" Effort and dedication will be required. Do what it takes to stay balanced, centered, and grounded. This is where you need to start. Living your life from a place of balance puts you closer to the divine.

MEDITATION

Meditation connects you to the divine. Daily meditation can raise your personal vibration. The benefits of meditation and self-Reiki are enormous for your health and wellbeing. This can be done in a traditional lotus position. It can also be done in savasana. It can be done anywhere and at any time. Express your intention. It is all about your intention.

1. *Say open.* This opens the crown chakra and lets the light in.
2. *Say input.* The word *input* directs the light to your core.
3. *Say restore.* The word *restore* gives the light purpose.
4. *Say balance.* This creates personal and energetic balance.
5. *Say grounding.* This will ground you to the earth and provide stabilization. Grounding will also increase your personal vibration and expansion. This provides an opportunity for docking and more expansion.
6. *Say thank you.* This expresses your gratitude for God's light.

Say each of these three times in a row, and then move on to the next one. Repeat as you desire.

Note: Each meditation is unique and divine. There should be no judging or comparison. Be a witness.

Note: Reiki practitioners can say and visualize the Reiki symbols during the meditation.

DAILY TIPS

Create a trusting, supportive, and valid relationship with self. This represents your relationship with God. Make sure it is a good one! Be your own best friend.

1. Follow the Reiki principles below.

   - Just for today, I will not worry.
   - Just for today, I will not be angry.
   - Just for today, I will be happy and free.
   - I will work hard on my spiritual growth and earn my living honestly.
   - I will honor and be kind to my parents, teachers, elders, and neighbors.
   - I will respect the oneness of all life.
   - I will count my blessings with gratitude.

2. Ask for assistance and guidance on a daily basis.
3. Read the words of *Ivo Speaks* on a daily basis.
4. Practice meditation/self-Reiki on a daily basis.
5. Practice a moving meditation like yoga on a daily basis.
6. Exercise proper thoughts and actions to stay balanced and centered.
7. Practice grounding to increase your personal vibration and expansion.
8. Shine your *light,* and be a servant of All That Is.

THE END

What you see, feel and hear around you is divine. It's a magical paradise where everything has a specific place and purpose. The world is not a crazy place but a highly organized and divinely orchestrated symphony. It's a masterpiece and we are the actors playing parts for the greater good. We are here to increase our vibration with each new life and raise the consciousness of the planet.

Agreements and promises are made with the divine prior to the arrival of each soul. The higher the soul, the fewer restrictions. Newer souls often need more guidelines and supervision. The divine selects the soul best suited for each human and family setting. There are no accidents on who ends up where. Family dynamics provide great opportunities to learn, grow and evolve. Responses with love and understanding to life's challenges increase one's good karma. Some of us, when faced with fear and anger, respond in a non pure way. This creates bad karma. Responses filled with love and compassion for yourself and others will increase your energetic vibration.

Your soul and the divine have their own agenda for your current incarnation. In many situations you are just along for the ride as they call the shots. Try to control your thoughts, feelings and emotions to minimize pain and suffering in your life. Loving thoughts and actions for yourself and others are in your best interest. Collecting good karma can pay off karmic debt and allow one to evolve to a higher position, status and capacity.

A review process takes place after death where each soul revisits his or her life from the perspective of those impacted. This can be a blissful or painful experience depending on the thoughts and actions of each soul during his or her life. Each soul will feel the love they shared and bestowed on others as well as any pain and discomfort. There is no action or thought in one's life that is not remembered by the divine. Think and act in a loving, caring and compassionate manner each and every day. Be your best self. You and the planet will experience the blessings of your purity.

You are encouraged by your guides and angels to fulfill your promises and agreements, to stay on your path, hopefully growing and evolving with each life toward greater enlightenment. The end game is a planet of enlightened beings. Everything is divine. We are all One!

Thank you for allowing me to share my story and the wisdom of Ivo. Remember:

- You are a divine, radiant being of light.
- You are an eternal spirit.
- Love is your essence.
- You are here to mature as a soul.
- You are here to become more enlightened.
- The endgame is a planet of enlightened souls.

Exercise your free will. Create and maintain greater balance in your life. Become more enlightened. As Ivo said, *"You can take a train or a missile; the choice is yours."*

Namaste
We are All One
With Light
Dane Boggs

Ivo

God is not a concept. God is within you.
All that is, is within you. It's all self-possessed.

With an open mind and a trusting heart, accept all
gracefully.

REIKI TESTIMONIALS

I would be fibbing if I didn't say I was a bit skeptical the first time I tried Reiki. I struggled to grasp the concept and questioned even more so, the effectiveness over the phone. I lead an active lifestyle, and generally have no complaints with my energy level...however I have had several dreadfully stressful events in my life over the past few years and was looking for an avenue to minimize the negative effects of stress from accumulating in me. After my first session with Dane, I was not only overwhelmed with the results....but was shocked by the outcome. With no prior knowledge, Dane pinpointed the source of my weakness...and the day after, I had a feeling of total mental and physical exhaustion that could not be explained. This day, my analogy is that it was like all the anguish was leaving....then a gradual refreshing feeling came to me over the course of the next day. Since last May, I have had several sessions with Dane over the phone and feel that they are just as effective as the live session, each is unique in it's own way. Another memorable outcome was me falling asleep in all my clothes....I did not wake up until the next morning. In my 50 years, I don't believe I have ever fallen asleep in my clothes. It is undoubtedly an overwhelming experience, and continues to surprise me with the effects.
MJ

Hope you were sending or I received from someone else. Had 2 rapid heart palpitations in the first few minutes, had a lot of flashing white light, star burst, then some light red and orange. Also to start my hands were real warm! Then I went to sleep. Also felt a bit nauseous, when I got up. I needed some sugar in my system so I drank some juice. Then I taught yoga class for 1 1/2 hours and it was awesome. Forgot to tell you I also saw different shapes of eyes during the session, like they were watching me in a safe way. Into the pure divine white light of the universe may your negative thoughts and feelings go, lead a pure and simple life.
Madie

Dane Boggs

I am amazed by Reiki. I wasn't quite sure what to make of Reiki when I first really learned of it a few years ago and would have to say I was slightly cynical. After months of chronic pain, and then receiving a Crohn's disease diagnosis, I was reeling physically and mentally, trying to deal with the pain and associated discomfort and attempting to get my mind around a lifelong incurable disease and the changes that were going to result. I saw Dane a few days after diagnosis and felt the pain subsiding quickly during the session and felt so much better afterward. Reiki reduced the pain greatly and enabled me to relax a bit and finally rest. Subsequent treatments have continued to lessen the pain and also help some of the drug side effects to subside. I also feel much more capable of working through the emotional issues of the disease. I am truly blessed that Dane found this path and is able to truly help so many of us.
Anonymous

Dane has treated me for everything from joint pain and asthma to vertigo and insomnia; a lifetime challenge. All with equal success. I have experienced a significant and on going reduction in joint pain, better balance, easier breathing and immediate and peaceful sleep. I have found Reiki to be a powerful healing force both physically and spiritually. So much so, that Dane as a Reiki Master has taught me to do Reiki. Dane has truly found his path as a gifted healer.
Patricia

My name is Abbey and I am from SLC, UT. I had the pleasure of meeting Reiki Master Dane Boggs while he was in town from Florida a few weeks back. I recently was involved in a horrible car accident that left major trauma in my body. Since the accident, I have not only suffered physical trauma but also depression. Introduced to Reiki for the first time by Dane, I was skeptical. He assured me that this form of healing helps many people with different types of conditions. Through his kindness I was given a free Reiki treatment. I had immediate results! I could not believe the way that it made me feel. I could describe it as someone taking a dark cloud out from my head and turning it into sun. The effects lasted the entire day. I have not felt this well in a long time. This amazing treatment has made me believe that I belong on the Reiki path. I am now working through Dane to get my attunements, and plan on becoming a Reiki Master one day.

Thank you Dane for your magic. You truly have a gift to share and I hope you touch many more lives, just the way you touched my life.
Abbey

The long distance session really helped last night. Very quickly after we hung up the phone, I felt what I can only describe as a compression of my upper left torso. My heart was pounding, it became a little harder to breathe (not alarming though), everything seemed to be pulsing in that area. This lasted for a good 5 min or so. I found it very interesting that every time I get pain in my left ankle. I've been telling the doctors for several years now since my last surgery that something is not right in there. This seems to be proving my theory. Other than some interesting feelings on three distinct points of my jaw (both sides and my chin), which made me concentrate on relaxing as I have TMJ and those are points where I tighten up. The biggest breakthrough is that whatever happened last night did more good than all the medicine I've had over the last week!!!! YIPPIE!!! My stomach no longer looks like I'm six months pregnant! I still have discomfort in my ribcage but I would expect that after all the irritation it has endured because of the strong medicines I've had to take.
Linda

Our 2 year old dog, Jorgan, had a life threatening liver problem. We decided to subject him to an operation that would potentially resolve all his issues. The operation was successful but 2 days later he developed seizures. The seizures are generally fatal. Fortunately Jorgan had help, Reiki Master Boggs, sent him Reiki nearly every day for about a week. With a terrible prognosis, he still somehow survived against the expectations of the vets. We attribute his return from the edge to his Reiki sessions. There is no medical explanation. We are so thankful to have our running dog back with us. Thank you Dane for bringing Reiki into our lives!
John

REIKI, to me, is a wonderful gift to all…humans, animals and the earth. I've known about it for a long time but I guess the time was not right for me to learn and go further. I had a surgery many years ago that was very hard to come back from. Many weeks in to the healing process a friend gave me a Reiki session. After weeks of pain I felt the change, the healing… and I was a believer. I went to a Reiki seminar… but as I said, I did not go further. I have worked with people all my life, educating and training them to become physically fit. It seemed a natural progression to include Reiki as part of my program…and yet I did not go further. More surgeries, a few more body wrenching accidents later …I woke up one day and said … "I need to get involved in Reiki"…once and for al! But who to learn from? I did my research, looked in to programs offered here in Pittsburgh, read bios, talked to people, studied websites…and I did not go further… One day I was on my computer. I wasn't researching ANYTHING to do with Reiki……and Dane's website just "appeared". I've gone over this a dozen times to figure out how looking on a site for horse supplements got me to visit Dane's website…but it did. I did something unusual for me. I actually took the time to read everything he had posted. I knew immediately that this was who I wanted to learn from. I couldn't decide on any other Reiki Master because Dane was my Reiki Master! I just need to find him!!! I DID go Further! I just received my level Three attunement and will definitely try to be a Reiki Master. There are such wonderful gifts given to us all thru Reiki as I said earlier. The more of us that GO FURTHER … I am so happy that Dane was put on my path. Thank you for being where I needed to find you.

Missy

AUTHOR

Dane was born in Charlottesville, Virginia and raised in Salt Lake City, Utah where he graduated from the University of Utah with a Bachelor of Science Degree. After college he purchased and remodeled homes in Pittsburgh before settling in Jacksonville in 1981. He started Boggs Construction Co. in 1983 where he remodeled and built custom homes in Jacksonville Florida until 2006.

In 2002, Dane began having health problems and was diagnosed with Huntington's disease. Fortunately his issues were not HD at the time but Lyme disease. Dane was diagnosed with Lyme Disease in 2004 and used oral antibiotics for one year and although he improved, he was still sick. He then used intravenous antibiotics for a second year. They also helped him but not enough to beat the disease. As he says, "A stalemate had been reached between the Lyme and myself". He knew he had to try something different and he started using an Electrical Frequency Generator -Rife machine. Using certain (low–frequency electromagnetic fields) for Lyme he became much healthier.

In 2009 he and his wife Aimee established the Northeast Florida Lyme Association - NEFLA with a few friends and Lyme Disease sufferers. NEFLA's mission was to improve the prevention, diagnosis, and successful treatment of Lyme and related vector borne diseases through education of the public and healthcare providers. In 2014 NEFLA became the FLDA - the Florida Lyme Disease Association. At that time Dane resigned to pursue his passions of Rife and Reiki full time.

Along the way Dane acquired his 200 hour yoga certification, additionally he trained with Pragata learning the 6 Lohan Qi Gong Method and received certification from Master Hong Liu in body pyramid. He trained with Laurelle Gaia and Michael Baird in Sedona Arizona becoming a

Reiki Master with Amy Layh in Jacksonville Florida. His Reiki Awakening occurred in 2007. He met his spiritual teacher Ivo in 2008. His book, "Reiki Awakening" chronicles his spiritual journey and the wisdom of Ivo.

Since 2016 Dane has been treating his Huntington's disease with positive results on the Rife machine. His ability to muscle test MT has allowed him to design a specific treatment plan for himself and others. "MT allows people to design a treatment program that is efficient and safe. It's important to know what frequencies to run, how long and the proper power setting, otherwise the Rife machine may not be very effective."

Dane continues to offer his services to others. Dane believes we do not need to suffer as we do. "Amazing things can happen when you tap into the healing energy of the universe with Rife and Reiki." He and his wife Aimee live in Ponte Vedra Beach, Florida.

APPENDICES FOR LYME DISEASE AND HUNTINGTON'S DISEASE

FOREWORD

Dane Boggs is a magnificent healer! Dane has used his incredible intuition and consciousness to create protocols for Lyme disease and Huntington's disease to be used on Rife machines. Dane has generously shared his protocols and wisdom to help all heal! I am honored for Dane's help in expanding my abilities to use the Rife machine. We, all people, are so lucky Dane has shared his experience and vast knowledge with Lyme disease and Huntington's disease.

Constance Wulf Acupuncture Physician
acuwulf.com

Disclaimer

Rife machines are not medical devices and are not approved by the FDA. The use of Rife technology is experimental and at your own risk. If you decide to experiment with Rife machines, please consult with your trusted licensed physician, as well as a professional electrician or electrical engineer. The efficacy of Rife machines to treat Lyme disease and Huntington's disease is unproven. There are no published, peer-reviewed, controlled studies on the effectiveness of this technology in treating these diseases. Using any form of Rife disease therapy can cause a Jarisch-Herxheimer reaction, known as a healing reaction. These reactions can be serious and/or fatal. Any Rife machine user assumes the risk of a severe Jarisch-Herxheimer

Dane Boggs

reaction. Neither the author nor the publisher accepts any responsibility for the reader's use of Rife technology and Rife machines.

LYME DISEASE

By The International Lyme and Associated Diseases Society

1.1

Lyme disease is transmitted by the bite of a tick, and the disease is prevalent across the United States and throughout the world. Ticks know no borders and respect no boundaries. A patient's county of residence does not accurately reflect his or her Lyme disease risk because people travel, pets travel, and ticks travel. This creates a dynamic situation with many opportunities for exposure to Lyme disease for each individual.

2.2

Lyme disease is a clinical diagnosis. The disease is caused by a spiral-shaped bacteria (spirochete) called Borrelia Burgdorferi. The Lyme spirochete can cause infection of multiple organs and produce a wide range of symptoms. Case reports in the medical literature document the protean manifestations of Lyme disease, and familiarity with its varied presentations is key to recognizing disseminated disease.

3.3

Fewer than 50% of patients with Lyme disease recall a tick bite. In some studies this number is as low as 15% in culture-proven infection with the Lyme spirochete.

4.4

Fewer than 50% of patients with Lyme disease recall any rash. Although the erythema migrans (EM) or "bull's-eye" rash is considered classic, it is not the most common dermatologic manifestation of early-localized Lyme infection. Atypical forms of this rash are seen far more commonly. It is important to know that the EM rash is pathognomonic of Lyme disease and requires no further verification prior to starting an appropriate course of antibiotic therapy.

5.5

The Centers For Disease Control And Prevention (CDC) surveillance criteria for Lyme disease were devised to track a narrow band of cases for epidemiologic purposes. **As stated on the CDC website, the surveillance criteria were never intended to be used as diagnostic criteria,** nor were they meant to define the entire scope of Lyme disease.

6.6

The elisa screening test is unreliable. The test misses 35% of culture proven Lyme disease (only 65% sensitivity) and is unacceptable as the first step of a two-step screening protocol. By definition, a screening test should have at least 95% sensitivity.

7.7

Of patients with acute culture-proven Lyme disease, 20–30% remain seronegative on serial western blot sampling. Antibody titers also appear to decline over time; thus while the western blot may remain positive for months, it may not always be sensitive enough to detect chronic infection with the Lyme spirochete. For "epidemiological purposes" the CDC eliminated from the western blot analysis the reading of bands 31 and 34. These bands are so specific to Borrelia Burgdorferi that they were chosen for vaccine development. Since a vaccine for Lyme disease is currently unavailable, however, a positive 31 or 34 band is highly indicative of Borrelia Burgdorferi exposure. Yet these bands are not reported in commercial Lyme tests.

8.8

When used as part of a diagnostic evaluation for Lyme disease, the western blot should be performed by a laboratory that reads and reports all of the bands related

to Borrelia Burgdorferi. Laboratories that use FDA approved kits (for instance, the mardx marblot®) are restricted from reporting all of the bands, as they must abide by the rules of the manufacturer. These rules are set up in accordance with the CDC's surveillance criteria and increase the risk of false-negative results. The commercial kits may be useful for surveillance purposes, but they offer too little information to be useful in patient management.

9.9
There are 5 subspecies of Borrelia Burgdorferi, over 100 strains in the USA, and 300 strains worldwide. This diversity is thought to contribute to the antigenic variability of the spirochete and its ability to evade the immune system and antibiotic therapy, leading to chronic infection.

10.10
Testing for Babesia, Anaplasma, Ehrlichia and Bartonella (other tick-transmitted organisms) should be performed. The presence of co-infection with these organisms points to probable infection with the Lyme spirochete as well. If these coinfections are left untreated, their continued presence increases morbidity and prevents successful treatment of Lyme disease.

11.11
A preponderance of evidence indicates that active **ongoing spirochetal infection with or without other tick-borne coinfections is the cause of the persistent symptoms in chronic Lyme disease.**

12.12
There has never been a study demonstrating that 30 days of antibiotic treatment cures chronic Lyme disease. However there is a plethora of documentation in the us and european medical literature demonstrating by histology and culture techniques that short courses of antibiotic treatment fail to eradicate the Lyme spirochete. Short treatment courses

have resulted in upwards of a 40% relapse rate, especially if treatment is delayed.

13.13

Most cases of chronic Lyme disease require an extended course of antibiotic therapy to achieve symptomatic relief. The return of symptoms and evidence of the continued presence of Borrelia Burgdorferi indicates the need for further treatment. The very real consequences of untreated chronic persistent Lyme infection far outweigh the potential consequences of long-term antibiotic therapy.

14.14

Many patients with chronic Lyme disease require prolonged treatment until the patient is symptom-free. Relapses occur and retreatment may be required. There are no tests currently available to prove that the organism is eradicated or that the patient with chronic Lyme disease is cured.

15.15

Like Syphilis in the 19th century, Lyme disease has been called the great imitator and should be considered in the differential diagnosis of rheumatologic and neurologic conditions, as well as Chronic Fatigue Syndrome, Fibromyalgia, Somatization Disorder and any difficult-to-diagnose multi-system illness.

Disclaimer: The foregoing information is for educational purposes only. It is not intended to replace or supersede patient care by a healthcare provider. If an individual suspects the presence of a tick-borne illness, that individual should consult a healthcare provider who is familiar with the diagnosis and treatment of tick-borne diseases.

- See more at: http://www.ilads.org/lyme/about-lyme.php#st hash.0U8c1zEr.dpuf

TREATMENT FREQUENCIES FOR LYME DISEASE AND COINFECTIONS

(Source - The New Universal Sideband Frequency List, Copyright 2017, By KD Enterprise LLC)

1-Lyme and Babesia: 693, 505, 2050, 1520, 615, 2016,485, 495, 254,128, 790, 864, 620, 630, 577, 4870, 2016, 4880, 578, 579, 610, 785, 795, 864, 7989, 1590, 239, 846, 422, 417, 76, 570, 1583, 1584, 753, 832, 5776, 18919.09, 941.93
2-Erlichia: 328, 336.4, 347, 366, 382.2, 385, 394.7, 672.7, 749.2, 764.4, 918, 1317, 1364.9, 1369.8
3-Lyme Hatchlings/Eggs: 640, 8554, 203, 412,414, 589, 667, 840, 1000, 1072, 1087, 1105
4-Bartonella-Cat Virus: 364, 379, 645, 654, 786, 840, 842, 844, 846, 848, 850, 857, 967, 6878, 634, 696, 716, 1518, 465
5-Chlamydia: 430, 620, 624, 840, 2213, 866, 471.6, 942.5, 1885.9, 3771.7, 7543.4, 470.5, 940, 1880, 3760.3, 7520.5, 3773, 3768, 2223, 2218, 942, 555, 943.3, 3767.3, 1111.4
6-Pneumonia Mycoplasma: 88, 975, 777, 2688, 660, 27400
7-Mycoplasma Pulmonis: 2404.2, 601, 300.5, 150.3, 75.1
7-Rocky Mountain Spotted Fever: 375, 862, 943, 788, 468, 308
8-Rickettsia: 129, 632, 943, 1062, 549, 547, 720, 726
9-Q Fever: 523, 1357, 607, 129, 632, 943, 1062, 549, 720, 726
10-Tularemia: 324, 427, 823, 3240, 8275, 32400
11-Toxoplasmosis: 434, 4340, 852, 8520
12-CMV Cytomegalovirus: 126, 597, 629, 682, 1045, 2145, 8848, 8856
13- Babesia: 76, 570, 1583, 1584, 432, 753, 5776

HUNTINGTON'S DISEASE

Huntington's disease (HD) is an inherited disorder that causes degeneration of brain cells, called neurons, in motor control regions of the brain, as well as other areas. Symptoms of the disease, which gets progressively worse, include uncontrolled movements (called chorea), abnormal body postures, and changes in behavior, emotion, judgment, and cognition. People with HD also develop impaired coordination, slurred speech, and difficulty feeding and swallowing. HD typically begins between ages 30 and 50. An earlier onset form called juvenile HD, occurs under age 20. Symptoms of juvenile HD differ somewhat from adult onset HD and include unsteadiness, rigidity, difficulty at school, and seizures. More than 30,000 Americans have HD.

Huntington's disease is caused by a mutation in the gene for a protein called huntingtin. The defect causes the cytosine, adenine, and guanine (CAG) building blocks of DNA to repeat many more times than is normal. Each child of a parent with HD has a 50-50 chance of inheriting the HD gene. If a child does not inherit the HD gene, he or she will not develop the disease and generally cannot pass it to subsequent generations. There is a small risk that someone who has a parent with the mutated gene but who did not inherit the HD gene may pass a possibly harmful genetic sequence to her/his children. A person who inherits the HD gene will eventually develop the disease. A genetic test, coupled with a complete medical history and neurological and laboratory tests, helps physicians diagnose HD.

There is no treatment that can stop or reverse the course of HD. Tetrabenazine is prescribed for treating Huntington's-associated chorea. It is the only drug approved by the U.S. Food and Drug Administration specifically for use against HD. Antipsychotic drugs may help to alleviate chorea and may also be used to help control hallucinations, delusions, and violent outbursts. Drugs may be prescribed to treat depression and anxiety. Drugs used to treat the symptoms of HD may have side effects such as fatigue, sedation, decreased concentration, restlessness, or hyperexcitability, and should be only used when symptoms create problems for the individual.[4]

---

[4] https://www.ninds.nih.gov/Disorders/All-Disorders/Huntingtons-Disease-Information-Page

Neuroscience Article

Neuroscience. 2012 May 3; 209:54-63. doi: 10.1016/j. neuroscience.2012.02.034. Epub 2012 Feb 25. Neuroprotective Effects Of Extremely Low-Frequency Electromagnetic Fields On A Huntington's Disease Rat Model: Effects On Neurotrophic Factors And Neuronal Density.

Tasset I1, Medina FJ, Jimena I, Agüera E, Gascón F, Feijóo M, Sánchez-López F, Luque E, Peña J, Drucker-Colín R, Túnez I.

Abstract

There is evidence to suggest that the neuroprotective effect of exposure of extremely low-frequency electromagnetic fields (ELF-EMF) may be due, at least in part, to the effect of these fields on neurotrophic factors levels and cell survival, leading to an improvement in behavior. This study was undertaken to investigate the neuroprotective effects of ELFEF in a rat model of 3-nitropropionic acid (3NP)-induced Huntington's disease. Behavior patterns were evaluated, and changes in neurotrophic factor, cell damage, and oxidative stress biomarker levels were monitored in Wistar rats. Rats were given 3NP over four consecutive days (20 mg/kg body weight), whereas ELFEF (60 Hz and 0.7 mT) was applied over 21 days, starting after the last injection of 3NP. Rats treated with 3NP exhibited significantly different behavior in the open field test (OFT) and the forced swim test (FST), and displayed significant differences in neurotrophic factor levels and oxidative stress biomarkers levels, together with a neuronal damage and diminished neuronal density, with respect neuronal controls. ELFEF improved neurological scores, enhanced neurotrophic factor levels, and reduced both oxidative damage and neuronal loss in 3NP-treated rats. ELFEF alleviates 3NP-induced brain injury and prevents loss of neurons in rat striatum, thus showing considerable potential as a therapeutic tool.

https://www.ncbi.nlm.nih.gov/pubmed/22406415

TREATMENT FREQUENCIES FOR HUNTINGTON'S DISEASE

(Source: The New Universal Sideband Frequency List, Copyright 2017, By KD Enterprise LLC)

Huntington's Disease Frequencies: 690, 484, 986, 430, 658, 744, 577, 275, 803, 660, 682, 322, 784, 880, 428, 764, 637, 657, 1565, 2, 728, 433, 528, 60.

TREATMENT FREQUENCIES FOR HUNTINGTON'S CHOREA
(Source: The New Universal Sideband Frequency List, Copyright 2017, By KD Enterprise LLC)

Huntington's Chorea Frequencies: 2250, 3910, 9750, 30800, 26125, 30167, 33333, 39877, 38183, 33860.

TREATMENT FREQUENCIES FOR HUNTINGTON'S DISEASE – AUTHOR'S STATEMENT

I am currently 66 with a 40 CAG HD repeat. The CAG repeat varies from 6 to 37 repeats on chromosomes of unaffected individuals and from more than 30 to 180 repeats on chromosomes of HD patients. The lower the CAG repeat number the slower the progression of the disease. In 2016 I started feeling out of sorts with anxiety issues and mood swings. I was on an emotional roller coaster and knew it was the HD. Fortunately I already had a Rife machine which I used to beat Lyme disease in 2008. I knew frequencies could kill Lyme spirochetes so why not use it to treat HD? Fortunately for me, the heavens delivered a Neuroscience article, "Neuroprotective Effects of Extremely Low-Frequency Electromagnetic Fields on A Huntington Disease Rat Model: Effects On Neurotropic Factors and Neuronal Density." The abstract shows considerable potential for extremely low-frequency electromagnetic fields as a therapeutic tool for Huntington's disease.

After reading the encouraging 2012 Neuroscience Article I Muscle Tested myself and found the frequencies for HD treatment. They are 690, 484, 986, 430, 658, 744, 577, 275, 803, 660, 682, 322, 784, 880, 428, 764,

637, 657, 1565, 2, 728, 433, 528, and 60. The frequencies were confirmed by a MT Kinesiologist. The frequencies for HD chorea are 2250, 3910, 9750, 30800, 26125, 30167, 33333, 39877, 38183 and 33860. These are found in The New Universal Sideband Frequency List from KD Enterprise LLC after 2018. I have been running these frequencies in various formats since 2016 with positive results. Some frequencies above may not be necessary and can be deleted. Some frequencies above may need to be repeated 2, 3, 4 or 5 times in a treatment session because they are so important. Most Rife machines allow you to pick a frequency, run it as many times as you desire with the gate on or off, at a particular hertz and Duty Cycle. They also allow you to select the power setting and the length of time. Please consider all the options available as you design your treatment protocol.

Rife Machines were developed by Dr Royal Raymond Rife in the 1930's. http://www.rifevideos.com/index.html. They produce radio waves that can treat all kinds of health issues. The New Universal Sideband Frequency List 2018 have frequencies for MS, Parkinson's, ALS, Alzheimer's and HD. Please remember that each Rife machine is different and requires training before experimentation. Try to find a gifted and qualified MT Kinesiologist to answer your particular questions. Monthly MT testing is recommended to maintain progress. Please explore other auto channels and frequencies in The New Universal Sideband Frequency in your fight against HD and other illnesses. The Rife machine has given me more time which is a wonderful gift. I feel it has delayed, reduced, minimized and slowed the progression of my disease. I encourage the HD community to use Rife technology (low -frequency electromagnetic fields) as a valuable tool to fight this disease.

The Rife machine has saved me time and time again. I am so blessed to still be here. Thank you God. Thank you All That Is. Thank you for bringing Reiki and Rife into my Life. Thank you for allowing me to be of Service. Blessings to you All.

Namaste
We are All One
With Light
Dane Boggs 2020

Printed in the United States
By Bookmasters